A History
of
Phallic Worship

A Discourse on the Worship of Priapus

A History of Phallic Worship
by Richard Payne Knight

Fredonia Books
Amsterdam, The Netherlands

A Discourse on the Worship of
Priapus
A History of Phallic Worship

by
Richard Payne Knight

ISBN 1-58963-036-X

Reprinted from the 1992 edition

Fredonia Books
Amsterdam, The Netherlands
http://www.FredoniaBooks.com

A DISCOURSE ON
THE WORSHIP OF PRIAPUS

AND ITS CONNECTION WITH THE
MYSTIC THEOLOGY OF THE ANCIENTS

BY

RICHARD PAYNE KNIGHT

TO WHICH IS ADDED
AN ACCOUNT OF THE REMAINS OF THE
WORSHIP OF PRIAPUS LATELY EXISTING
AT ISERNIA IN THE KINGDOM OF NAPLES

BY SIR WILLIAM HAMILTON, K. B.

WITH PLATES

PREFACE

RICHARD PAYNE KNIGHT, one of the most distinguished patrons of art and learning in England during his time, a scholar of great attainments, an eminent antiquarian, member of the Radical party in Parliament, and a writer of great ability, was born at Wormesley Grange, in Herefordshire, in 1750. From an early age he devoted himself to the study of ancient literature, antiquities, and mythology. A large portion of his inherited fortune was expended in the collection of antiquities, especially, ancient coins, medals, and bronzes. His collection, which was continued until his death in 1820, was bequeathed to the British Museum, and accepted for that institution by a special act of Parliament. Its value was estimated at £50,000.

Among his works are an *Inquiry into the Principles of Taste; Analytical Essay on the Greek Alphabet; The Symbolical Language of Ancient Art;* and three poems; *The Landscape, the Progress of Civil Society,* and *The Romance of Alfred.*

The *Worship of Priapus* was originally printed in
1786. The bold utterances of Mr. Knight on a subject
which until that time had been entirely tabooed, or
had been treated in a way to hide rather than to discover the truth, shocked the sensibilities of the higher
classes of English society, and the ministers and
members of the various denominations of the Christian world. Rather than endure the storm of criti-
cism, aroused by the publication, he suppressed
during his lifetime all the copies of the book he
could recall, consequently it became very scarce, and
has continued so.

The numerous illustrations are engraved from antique coins, medals, stone carvings, etc., preserved in
the Payne Knight collection in the British Museum.
These are only to be found in museums and private
collections scattered over Europe, and are practically
inaccessible to the student; they are here engraved
and fully described.

The present edition is published in the interest of
science and scholarship. At a time when so many
learned investigators are endeavouring to trace back
religious beliefs and practices to their origin, it would
seem that this is a branch of the subject which should
not be ignored. The history of religions has been
studied with more zeal and success during the nine-
teenth and twentieth centuries, than in all the ages

which preceded them, and this book has now an interest fifty fold greater than when originally published.

The short account of the Remains of the Worship of Priapus in the Kingdom of Naples is from the letter of Sir William Hamilton, K.B., His Majesty's Minister at the Court of Naples, to Sir Joseph Banks, Bart., then President of the Royal Society.

ON THE WORSHIP OF PRIAPUS
IN THE KINGDOM OF NAPLES

Sir,   *Naples, Dec. 30, 1781.*

HAVING last year made a curious discovery,
that in a Province of this Kingdom, and not
fifty miles from its Capital, a sort of devotion
is still paid to PRIAPUS, the obscene Divinity of the
Ancients (though under another denomination), I
thought it a circumstance worth recording; particularly, as it offers a fresh proof of the similitude of
the Popish and Pagan Religion, so well observed by
Dr. Middleton, in his celebrated Letter from Rome:
and therefore I mean to deposit the authentic [1] proofs
of this assertion in the British Museum, when a
proper opportunity shall offer. In the meantime I
send you the following account, which, I flatter myself, will amuse you for the present, and may in
future serve to illustrate those proofs.

I had long ago discovered, that the women and

[1] A specimen of each of the *ex-voti* of wax, with the original
letter from Isernia. See the Ex-voti, Plate I.

children of the lower class, at Naples, and in its neighbourhood, frequently wore, as an ornament of dress, a sort of Amulets, (which they imagine to be a preservative from the *mal occhii, evil eyes,* or enchantment) exactly similar to those which were worn by the ancient Inhabitants of this Country for the very same purpose, as likewise for their supposed invigorating influence; and all of which have evidently a relation to the Cult of Priapus. Struck with this conformity in ancient and modern superstition, I made a collection of both the ancient and modern Amulets of this sort, and placed them together in the British Museum, where they remain. The modern Amulet most in vogue represents a hand clinched, with the point of the thumb thrust betwixt the index and middle [1] finger; the next is a shell; and the third is a half-moon. These Amulets (except the shell, which is usually worn in its natural state) are most commonly made of silver, but sometimes of ivory, coral, amber, crystal, or some curious gem, or pebble. We have a proof of the hand above described having a connection with Priapus, in a most elegant small idol of bronze of that Divinity, now in the Royal Museum of Portici, and which was found in the ruins of Herculaneum: it has an enormous Phallus, and, with an

---

[1] See Plate ii., Fig. 1.

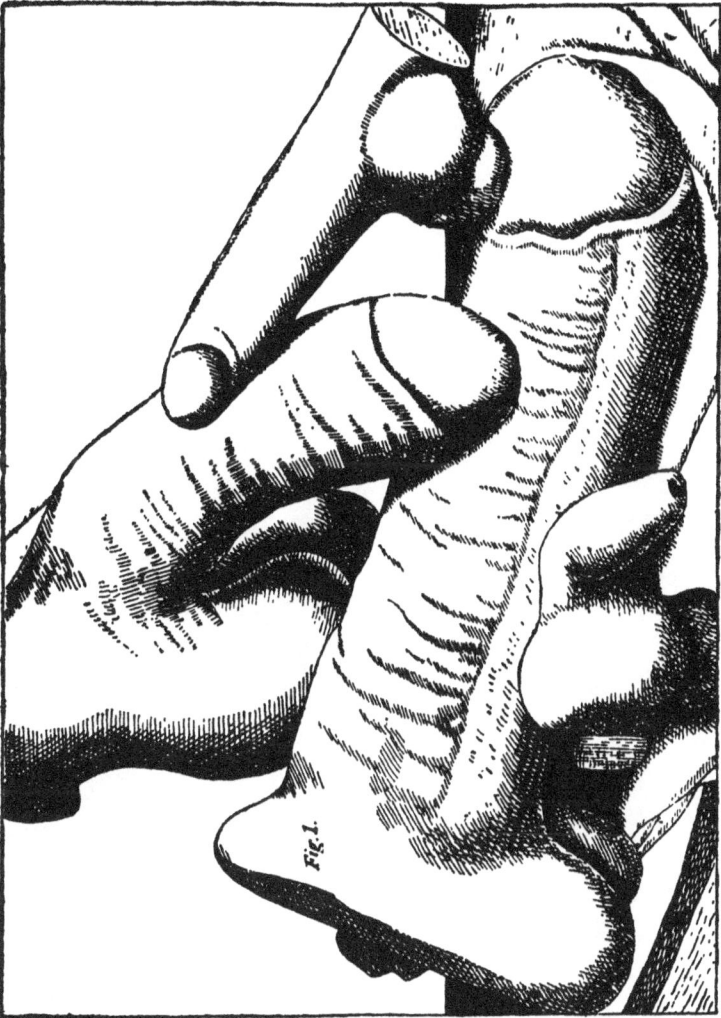

PLATE I

EX VOTI OF WAX. FROM ISERNIA

arch look and gesture, stretches out its right hand in the form above mentioned; [1] and which probably was an emblem of consummation: and as a further proof of it, the Amulet which occurs most frequently amongst those of the Ancients (next to that which represents the simple Priapus), is such a hand united with the Phallus; of which you may see several specimens in my collection in the British Museum. One in particular, I recollect, has also the half-moon joined to the hand and Phallus; which half-moon is supposed to have an allusion to the female *menses.* The shell, or *concha veneris*, is evidently an emblem of the female part of generation. It is very natural then to suppose, that the Amulets representing the Phallus alone, so visibly indecent, may have been long out of use in this civilized capital; but I have been assured, that it is but very lately that the Priests have put an end to the wearing of such Amulets in Calabria, and other distant Provinces of this Kingdom.

A new road having been made last year from this Capital to the Province of Abruzzo, passing through the City of Isernia (anciently belonging to the Samnites, and very populous [2]), a person of liberal education, employed in that work, chanced to be at

[1] In the first volume of the Bronzes of the Herculaneum.
[2] The actual population of Isernia is 5156.

Isernia just at the time of the celebration of the Feast of the modern Priapus, St. Cosmo; and having been struck with the singularity of the ceremony, so very similar to that which attended the ancient Cult of the God of the Gardens, and knowing my taste for antiquities, told me of it. From this Gentleman's report, and from what I learnt on the spot from the Governor of Isernia himself, having gone to that city on purpose in the month of February last, I have drawn up the following account, which I have reason to believe is strictly true. I did intend to have been present at the Feast of St. Cosmo this year; but the indecency of this ceremony having probably trans-pired, from the country's having been more fre-quented since the new road was made, orders have been given, that the *Great Toe* [1] of the Saint should no longer be exposed. The following is the account of the Fête of St. Cosmo and Damiano, as it actually was celebrated at Isernia, on the confines of Abruzzo, in the Kingdom of Naples, so late as in the year of our Lord 1780.

On the 27th of September, at Isernia, one of the most ancient cities of the Kingdom of Naples, situ-ated in the Province called the Contado di Molise, and adjoining to Abruzzo, an annual Fair is held,

---

[1] It appears the modern Priapi were so called at Isernia.

PLATE II

ANCIENT AND MODERN AMULETS

which lasts three days. The situation of this Fair is on a rising ground, between two rivers, about half a mile from the town of Isernia; on the most elevated part of which there is an ancient church, with a vestibule. The architecture is of the style of the lower ages; and it is said to have been a church and convent belonging to the Benedictine Monks in the time of their poverty. This church is dedicated to St. Cosmus and Damianus. One of the days of the Fair, the relicks of the Saints are exposed, and afterwards carried in procession from the cathedral of the city to this church, attended by a prodigious concourse of people. In the city, and at the fair, *ex-voti* of wax, representing the male parts of generation, of various dimensions, some even of the length of the palm, are publickly offered to sale. There are also waxen vows, that represent other parts of the body mixed with them; but of these there are few in comparison of the number of the Priapi. The devout distributers of these vows carry a basket full of them in one hand, and hold a plate in the other to receive the money, crying aloud, "St. Cosmo and Damiano!" If you ask the price of one, the answer is, *più ci metti, più meriti:* "The more you give, the more's the merit." In the vestibule are two tables, at each of which one of the canons of the church presides, this crying out, *Qui si riceveno le Misse, e Litanie:* "Here Masses and

Litanies are received; " and the other, *Qui si riceveno li Voti:* "Here the Vows are received." The price of a Mass is fifteen Neapolitan grains, and of a Litany five grains. On each table is a large bason for the reception of the different offerings. The Vows are chiefly presented by the female sex; and they are seldom such as represent legs, arms, &c., but most commonly the male parts of generation. The person who was at this fête in the year 1780, and who gave me this account (the authenticity of every article of which has since been fully confirmed to me by the Governor of Isernia), told me also, that he heard a woman say, at the time she presented a Vow, like that which is presented in Plate 1, Fig. i., *Santo Cosimo benedetto, cosi lo voglio:* "Blessed St. Cosmo, let it be like this; " another, *St. Cosimo, a te mi raccommendo:* "St. Cosmo, I recommend myself to you; " and a third, *St. Cosimo, ti ringrazio:* "St. Cosmo, I thank you." The Vow is never presented without being accompanied by a piece of money, and is always kissed by the devotee at the moment of presentation.

At the great altar in the church, another of its canons attends to give the holy unction, with the oil of St. Cosmo;[1] which is prepared by the same re-

[1] The cure of diseases by oil is likewise of ancient date; for

ceipt as that of the Roman Ritual, with the addition only of the prayer of the Holy Martyrs, St. Cosmus and Damianus. Those who have an infirmity in any of their members, present themselves at the great altar, and uncover the member affected (not even excepting that which is most frequently represented by the *ex-voti*); and the reverend canon anoints it, saying, *Per intercessionem beati Cosmi, liberet te ab omni malo. Amen.*

The ceremony finishes by the canons of the church dividing the spoils, both money and wax, which must be to a very considerable amount, as the concourse at this fête is said to be prodigiously numerous.

The oil of St. Cosmo is in high repute for its invigorating quality, when the loins, and parts adjacent, are anointed with it. No less than 1400 flasks of that oil were either expended at the altar in unctions, or charitably distributed, during this fête in the year 1780; and as it is usual for every one, who either makes use of the oil at the altar, or carries off a flask of it, to leave an alms for St. Cosmo, the ceremony of the oil becomes likewise a very lucrative one to the canons of the church.

Tertullian tells us, that a Christian, called Proculus, cured the Emperor Severus of a certain distemper by the use of oil; for which service the Emperor kept Proculus, as long as he lived, in his palace.

ON THE WORSHIP OF PRIAPUS

MEN, considered collectively, are at all times
the same animals, employing the same organs, and endowed with the same faculties:
their passions, prejudices, and conceptions, will of
course be formed upon the same internal principles,
although directed to various ends, and modified in
various ways, by the variety of external circumstances operating upon them. Education and science
may correct, restrain, and extend; but neither can
annihilate or create: they may turn and embellish
the currents; but can neither stop nor enlarge the
springs, which, continuing to flow with a perpetual
and equal tide, return to their ancient channels, when
the causes that perverted them are withdrawn.

The first principles of the human mind will be
more directly brought into action, in proportion to
the earnestness and affection with which it contem-
plates its object; and passion and prejudice will acquire dominion over it, in proportion as its first prin-

ciples are more directly brought into action. On all common subjects, this dominion of passion and prejudice is restrained by the evidence of sense and perception; but, when the mind is led to the contemplation of things beyond its comprehension, all such restraints vanish: reason has then nothing to oppose to the phantoms of imagination, which acquire terrors from their obscurity, and dictate uncontrolled, because unknown. Such is the case in all religious subjects, which, being beyond the reach of sense or reason, are always embraced or rejected with violence and heat. Men think they know, because they are sure they feel; and are firmly convinced, because strongly agitated. Hence proceed that haste and violence with which devout persons of all religions condemn the rites and doctrines of others, and the furious zeal and bigotry with which they maintain their own; while perhaps, if both were equally well understood, both would be found to have the same meaning, and only to differ in the modes of conveying it.

Of all the profane rites which belonged to the ancient polytheism, none were more furiously inveighed against by the zealous propagators of the Christian faith, than the obscene ceremonies performed in the worship of Priapus; which appeared not only contrary to the gravity and sanctity of religion, but subversive of the first principles of decency and good order in society. Even the form itself, under which the god was represented, appeared to them a mockery of all piety and devotion, and more fit to be placed in a brothel than a temple. But the forms and ceremonials of a religion are not always to be understood in their direct and obvious sense; but are to be considered as symbolical representations of some hidden meaning, which may be extremely wise and just, though the symbols themselves, to those who know not their true signification, may appear in the highest degree absurd and extravagant. It has often happened, that avarice and superstition have continued these symbolical representations for ages after their original meaning has been lost and forgotten; when they must of course appear nonsensical and ridiculous, if not impious and extravagant.

Such is the case with the rite now under consideration, than which nothing can be more monstrous and indecent, if considered in its plain and obvious meaning, or as a part of the Christian worship; but which will be found to be a very natural symbol of a very natural and philosophical system of religion, if considered according to its original use and intention.

What this was, I shall endeavour in the following sheets to explain as concisely and clearly as possible. Those who wish to know how generally the symbol, and the religion which it represented, once prevailed, will consult the great and elaborate work of Mr. D'Hancarville, who, with infinite learning and ingenuity, has traced its progress over the whole earth. My endeavour will be merely to show, from what original principles in the human mind it was first adopted, and how it was connected with the ancient theology: matters of very curious inquiry, which will serve, better perhaps than any others, to illustrate that truth, which ought to be present in every man's mind when he judges of the actions of others, *that in morals, as well as physics, there is no effect without an adequate cause.* If in doing this, I frequently find it necessary to differ in opinion with the learned author above-mentioned, it will be always with the utmost deference and respect; as it is to him that we are indebted for the only reasonable method of explaining the emblematical works of the ancient artists.

Whatever the Greeks and Egyptians meant by the symbol in question, it was certainly nothing ludicrous or licentious; of which we need no other proof, than its having been carried in solemn procession at the celebration of those mysteries in which the first principles of their religion, the knowledge of the God of Nature, the First, the Supreme, the Intellectual,[1] were

[1] Plut. *de Is, et Os.*

preserved free from the vulgar superstitions, and communicated, under the strictest oaths of secrecy, to the iniated (initiated); who were obliged to purify themselves, prior to their initiation, by abstaining from venery, and all impure food.[1] We may therefore be assured, that no impure meaning could be conveyed by this symbol; but that it represented some fundamental principle of their faith. What this was, it is difficult to obtain any direct information, on account of the secrecy under which this part of their religion was guarded. Plutarch tells us, that the Egyptians represented Osiris with the organ of generation erect, to show his generative and prolific power: he also tells us, that Osiris was the same Diety as the Bacchus of the Greek Mythology; who was also the same as the first begotten Love (Ερως πρωτογονος) of Orpheus and Hesiod.[2] This deity is celebrated by the ancient poets as the creator of all things, the father of gods and men;[3] and it appears, by the passage above referred to, that the organ of generation was the symbol of his great characteristic attribute. This is perfectly consistent with the general practice of the Greek artists, who (as will be made appear hereafter) uniformly represented the attributes of the deity by the corresponding proper-

[1] Plut. *de Is. et Os.*   [2] Ibid.   [3] Orph. *Argon.* 422.

ties observed in the objects of sight. They thus personified the epithets and titles applied to him in the hymns and litanies, and conveyed their ideas of him by forms, only intelligible to the initiated, instead of sounds, which were intelligible to all. The organ of generation represented the generative or creative attribute, and in the language of painting and sculpture, signified the same as the epithet παγγενετωζ, in the Orphic litanies.

This interpretation will perhaps surprise those who have not been accustomed to divest their minds of the prejudices of education and fashion; but I doubt not, but it will appear just and reasonable to those who consider manners and customs as relative to the natural causes which produced them, rather than to the artificial opinions and prejudices of any particular age or country. There is naturally no impurity or licentiousness in the moderate and regular gratification of any natural appetite; the turpitude consisting wholly in the excess or perversion. Neither are organs of one species of enjoyment naturally to be considered as subjects of shame and concealment more than those of another; every refinement of modern manners on this head being derived from acquired habit, not from nature: habit, indeed, long established; for it seems to have been as general in Homer's days as at present; but which certainly did not exist when the mystic symbols of the ancient worship were first adopted. As these symbols were intended to express abstract ideas by objects of sight, the contrivers of them naturally selected those objects whose characteristic properties seemed to have the greatest analogy with the Divine attributes which they wished to represent. In an age, therefore, when no prejudices of artificial decency existed, what more just and natural image could they find, by which to express their idea of the beneficent power of the great Creator, than that organ which endowed them with the power of procreation, and made them partakers, not only of the felicity of the Deity, but of his great characteristic attribute, that of multiplying his own image, communicating his blessings, and extending them to generations yet unborn?

In the ancient theology of Greece, preserved in the Orphic Fragments, this Deity, the Ερως πρωτογονος, or first-begotten Love, is said to have been produced, together with Æther, by Time, or Eternity (Κρονος), and Necessity (Αναγχη), operating upon inert matter (Χαος). He is described as eternally begetting (αειγνητης); the Father of Night, called in later times, the lucid or splendid, (φανης), because he first appeared in splendour; of a double nature, (διφνης), as possessing the general power of creation and generation, both active and passive, both male and female.[1] Light is his necessary and pri-

[1] Orph. *Argon.*, ver. 12. This poem of the Argonautic Expedition is not of the ancient Orpheus, but written in his name by some poet posterior to Homer; as appears by the allusion to Orpheus's descent into hell; a fable invented after the Homeric times. It is, however, of very great antiquity, as both the style and manner sufficiently prove; and, I think, cannot be later than the age of Pisistratus, to which it has been generally attributed. The passage here referred to is cited from another poem, which, at the time this was written, passed for a genuine work of the Thracian bard: whether justly or not, matters little; for its being thought so at that time proves it to be of the remotest antiquity. The other Orphic poems cited in this discourse are the Hymns, or Litanies, which are attributed by the early Christian and later Platonic writers to Onomacritus, a poet of the age of Pisistratus; but which are probably of various authors (See Brucker. *Hist. Crit. Philos.*, vol. i., part 2, lib i., c. i.) They contain, however, nothing which proves them to be later than the Trojan times; and if Onomacritus, or any later author, had anything to do with them, it seems to have been only in new-versifying them, and changing the dialect (See Gesner. *Proleg. Orphica*, p. 26). Had he forged them, and attempted to impose them upon the world, as the genuine compositions of an ancient bard, there can be no doubt but that he would have stuffed them with antiquated words and obsolete phrases; which is by no means the case, the language being pure and worthy the age of Pisistratus. These poems are not properly hymns, for the hymns of the Greeks contained the nativities and actions of the gods, like those of Homer and Callimachus; but these are compositions of a different kind, and are properly invocations or prayers used in the Orphic mysteries, and seem nearly of the same class as the Psalms of the Hebrews. The reason why they are so seldom mentioned by any of the early writers, and so perpetually referred to by the later, is that they belonged to the mystic worship, where everything was kept concealed under the strictest oaths of secrecy. But after the rise of Christianity, this sacred silence

was broken by the Greek converts, who revealed everything which they thought would depreciate the old religion or recommend the new; whilst the heathen priests revealed whatever they thought would have contrary tendency; and endeavoured to show, by publishing the real mystic creed of their religion, that the principles of it were not so absurd as its outward structure seemed to infer; but that, when stripped of poetical allegory and vulgar fable, their theology was pure, reasonable, and sublime (Gesner. *Proleg. Orphica*). The collection of these poems now extant, being probably compiled and versified by several hands, with some forged, and other interpolated and altered, must be read with great caution; more especially the Fragments preserved by the Fathers of the Church and Ammonian Platonics; for these writers made no scruple of forging any monuments of antiquity which suited their purposes; particularly the former, who, in addition to their natural zeal, having the interests of a confederate body to support, thought every means by which they could benefit that body, by extending the lights of revelation, and gaining proselytes to the true faith, not only allowable, but meritorious (See Clementina, Hom. vii., sec. 10. Recogn. lib. i., sec. 65. Origen, *apud Hieronom. Apolog. i., contra Ruf.* et Chrysostom. *de Sacerdot.*, lib. i. Chrysostom, in particular, not only justifies, but warmly commends, any frauds that can be practiced for the advantage of the Church of Christ). Pausanias says (lib. ix.), that the Hymns of Orpheus were few and short; but next in poetical merit to those of Homer, and superior to them in sanctity (ϑεολογικωτεροι) These are probably the same as the genuine part of the collection now extant; but they are so intermixed, that it is difficult to say which are genuine and which are not. Perhaps there is no surer rule for judging than to compare the epithets and allegories with the symbols and monograms on the Greek medals, and to make their agreement the test of authenticity. The medals were the public acts and records of the State, made under the direction of the magistrates, who were generally initiated into the mysteries. We may therefore be assured, that whatever theological and mythological allusions are found upon them were part of the ancient religion of Greece. It is from these that many of the Orphic Hymns and Fragments are proved to contain the pure theology or mystic faith of the ancients, which is called Orphic by Pausanias (lib. 1., c. 39), and which is so unlike the vulgar religion, or poetical mythology, that one can scarcely imagine at first sight that it belonged to the same people; but which will nevertheless appear, upon accurate investigation, to be the source from whence it flowed, and the cause of all its extravagance.

The history of Orpheus himself is so confused and obscured by fable, that it is impossible to obtain any certain information concerning him. According to general tradition, he was a Thracian, and introduced the mysteries, in which a more pure system of religion was taught, into Greece (Brucker, vol. i., part 2, lib. i., c. 1.) He is also said to have travelled into Egypt (Diodor. Sic. lib. i., p. 80); but as the Egyptians pretended that all foreigners received their sciences from them, at a time when all foreigners who entered the country were put to death or enslaved (Diodor. Sic. lib. i., pp. 78 et 107), this account may be rejected, with many others of the same kind. The Egyptians certainly could not have taught Orpheus the plurality of worlds, and true solar system, which appear to have been the fundamental principles of his philosophy and religion (Plutarch. *de Placit. Philos.*, lib. ii., c. 13. Brucker *in loc. citat.*) Nor could he have gained this knowledge from any people which history has preserved any memorials; for we know of none among whom science had made such a progress, that a truth so remote from common observation, and so contradictory to the evidence of unimproved sense, would not have been rejected, as it was by all the sects of Greek philosophy except the Pythagoreans, who rather revered it as an article of faith, than understood it as a discovery of science. Thrace was certainly inhabited by a civilized nation at some remote period; for, when Philip of Macedon opened the gold mines in that country, he found that they had been worked before with great expense and ingenuity, by a people well versed in mechanics, of whom no memorials whatever were then extant. Of these, probably, was Orpheus, as well as Thamyris, both of whose poems, Plato says, could be read with pleasure in his time.

mary attribute, co-eternal with himself, and with him brought forth from inert matter by necessity. Hence the purity and sanctity always attributed to light by the Greeks.[1] He is called the Father of Night, because by attracting the light to himself, and becoming the fountain which distributed it to the world, he produced night, which is called eternally-begotten, because it had eternally existed, although mixed and lost in the general mass. He is said to pervade the world with the motion of his wings, bringing pure light; and thence to be called the splendid, the ruling Priapus, and self-illumined (ανταvyης[2]). It is to be observed that the word Πριηπος, afterwards the name of a subordinate deity, is here used as a title relating to one of his attributes; the reasons for which I shall endeavour to explain hereafter. Wings are figuratively attributed to him as being the emblems of swiftness and incubation; by the first of which he pervaded matter, and by the second fructified the egg of Chaos. The egg was carried in procession at the celebration of the mysteries, because, as Plutarch says, it was the material of generation (νλη της γενεσεως[3]) containing the seeds and germs of life and motion, without being actually possessed of either.

[1] See Sophocl. *Œdip. Tyr.*, ver. 1436.
[2] Orph. Hym. 5.
[3] Symph. 1. 2.

For this reason, it was a very proper symbol of Chaos, containing the seeds and materials of all things, which, however, were barren and useless, until the Creator fructified them by the incubation of his vital spirit, and released them from the restraints of inert matter, by the efforts of his divine strength. The incubation of the vital spirit is represented on the colonial medals of Tyre, by a serpent wreathed around an egg; [1] for the serpent, having the power of casting his skin, and apparently renewing his youth, became the symbol of life and vigour, and as such is always made an attendant on the mythological deities presiding over health.[2] It is also observed, that animals of the serpent kind retain life more pertinaciously than any others except the Polypus, which is sometimes represented upon the Greek Medals,[3] probably in its stead. I have myself seen the heart of an adder continue its vital motions for many minutes after it has been taken from the body, and even renew them, after it has been cold, upon being moistened with warm water, and touched with a stimulus.

The Creator, delivering the fructified seeds of things from the restraints of inert matter by his divine

[1] See Plate XXI. Fig. 1.
[2] Macrob. Sat. i. c. 20.
[3] See Goltz, Tab. II. Figs. 7 and 8.

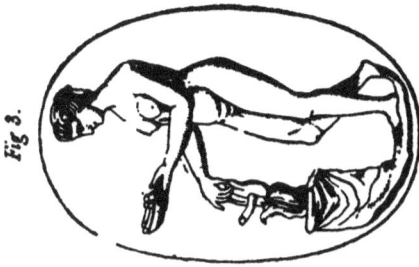

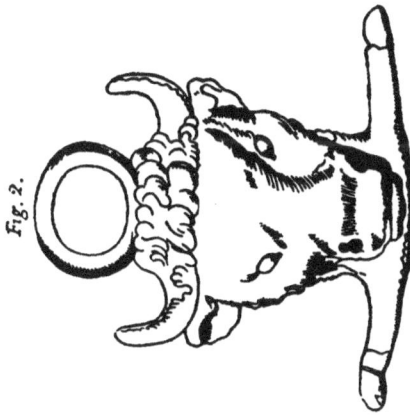

Fig. 3.

Fig. 2.

Fig. 1

Fig. 6

Fig. 5

Fig. 7.

Fig. 4

PLATE III

ANTIQUE GEMS AND GREEK MEDALS

strength, is represented on innumerable Greek medals by the Urus, or wild Bull, in the act of butting against the Egg of Chaos, and breaking it with his horns.[1] It is true, that the egg is not represented with the bull on any of those which I have seen; but Mr. D'Hancarville [2] has brought examples from other countries, where the same system prevailed, which, as well as the general analogy of the Greek theology, prove that the egg must have been understood, and that the attitude of the bull could have no other meaning. I shall also have occasion hereafter to show by other examples, that it was no uncommon practice, in these mystic monuments, to make a part of a group represent the whole. It was from this horned symbol of the power of the Deity that horns were placed in the portraits of kings to show that their power was derived from Heaven, and acknowledged no earthly superior. The moderns have indeed changed the meaning of this symbol, and given it a sense of which, perhaps, it would be difficult to find the origin, though I have often wondered that it has never exercised the sagacity of those learned gentle-

---

[1] See Plate IV. Fig. 1, and Recherches sur les Arts, vol. i. Pl. VIII. The Hebrew word *Chroub*, or *Cherub*, signified originally *strong* or *robust;* but is usually employed metaphorically, signifying a Bull. See Cleric. in *Exod*. c. xxv.

[2] Recherches sur les Arts, lib. i.

men who make British antiquities the subjects of their laborious inquiries. At present, it certainly does not bear any character of dignity or power; nor does it ever imply that those to whom it is attributed have been particularly favoured by the generative or creative powers. But this is a subject much too important to be discussed in a digression; I shall therefore leave it to those learned antiquarians who have done themselves so much honour, and the public so much service, by their successful inquiries into customs of the same kind. To their indefatigable industry and exquisite ingenuity I earnestly recommend it, only observing that this modern acceptation of the symbol is of considerable antiquity, for it is mentioned as proverbial in the Oneirocritics of Artemidorus; [1] and that it is not now confined to Great Britain, but prevails in most parts of Christendom, as the ancient acceptation of it did formerly in most parts of the world, even among that people from whose religion Christianity is derived; for it is a common mode of expression in the Old Testament, to say that the horns of any one shall be exalted, in order to signify that he shall be raised into power or pre-eminence; and when Moses descended from the Mount with the spirit of God still upon him, his head appeared horned.[2]

[1] Lib. 1. c. 12.

[2] *Exod.* c. xxxiv. v. 35, ed. Vulgat. Other translators under-

Fig. 1.

Fig. 2.

Fig. 3.

Fig. 4.

Fig. 5.

PLATE IV

MEDALS POSSESSED BY PAYNE KNIGHT

To the head of the bull was sometimes joined the organ of generation, which represented not only the strength of the Creator, but the peculiar direction of it to the most beneficial purpose, the propagation of sensitive beings. Of this there is a small bronze in the Museum of Mr. Townley, of which an engraving is given in Plate III. Fig. 2.[1]

Sometimes this generative attribute is represented by the symbol of the goat, supposed to be the most salacious of animals, and therefore adopted upon the same principles as the bull and the serpent.[2] The choral odes, sung in honour of the generator Bacchus, were hence called τραγωδιαι, or songs of the goat; a title which is now applied to the dramatic dialogues anciently inserted in these odes, to break their uniformity . On a medal, struck in honour of Augustus, the goat terminates in the tail of a fish, to show the generative power incorporated with water. Under his feet is the globe of the earth, supposed to be fertilised by this union; and upon his back, the cornucopia, representing the result of this fertility.[3]

---

stand the expression metaphorically, and suppose it to mean radiated, or luminous.

[1] See Plate III.

[2] Τον δε τραγον αωεθεωσαν (οι Αιγνωτιοι) καθαωερ και ωαρα τοις Ελλησι τετιησθαι λεγκσι τον Πριαωον, δια το γεννητιχον μοριον.   DIODOR. lib. 1. p. 78.

[3] Plate x. Fig. 3.

Mr. D'Hancarville attributes the origin of all these symbols to the ambiguity of words; the same term being employed in the primitive language to signify God and a Bull, the Universe and a Goat, Life and a Serpent. But words are only the types and symbols of ideas, and therefore must be posterior to them, in the same manner as ideas are to their objects. The words of a primitive language, being imitative of the ideas from which they sprung, and of the objects they meant to express, as far as the imperfections of the organs of speech will admit, there must necessarily be the same kind of analogy between them as between the ideas and objects themselves. It is impossible, therefore, that in such a language any ambiguity of this sort could exist, as it does in secondary languages; the words of which, being collected from various sources, and blended together without having any natural connection, become arbitrary signs of convention, instead of imitative representations of ideas. In this case it often happens, that words, similar in form, but different in meaning, have been adopted from different sources, which, being blended together, lose their little difference of form, and retain their entire difference of meaning. Hence ambiguities arise, such as those above mentioned, which could not possibly exist in an original tongue.

The Greek poets and artists frequently give the personification of a particular attribute for the Deity himself; hence he is called Ταυροζοας, Ταυρωπος, Ταυρομορφος,[1] &c., and hence the initials and monograms of the Orphic epithets applied to the Creator, are found with the bull, and other symbols, on the Greek medals.[2] It must not be imagined from hence, that the ancients supposed the Deity to exist under the form of a bull, a goat, or a serpent: on the contrary, he is always described in the Orphic theology as a general pervading Spirit, without form, or distinct locality of any kind; and appears, by a curious fragment preserved by Proclus,[3] to have been no other than *attraction* personified. The self-created mind (νοος αυτογενεθλος) of the Eternal Father is said to have spread the heavy bond of love through all things (πασιν ενεοπειρεν δεσμον περιζριθη Ερωτος), in order that they might endure for ever. This Eternal Father is Κρονος, time or eternity, personified; and so taken for the unknown Being that fills eternity and infinity. The ancient theologists knew that we could form no positive idea of infinity, whether of power, space, or time; it being

[1] Orph. Hymn. v. et xxix.
[2] Numm. Vet. Pop. et Urb. Tab. xxxix. Figs 19 et 20. They are on most of the medals of Marseilles, Naples, Thurium and many other cities.
[3] In *Tim.* iii., et *Frag. Orphic.*, ed. Gesner.

fleeting and fugitive, and eluding the understanding by a continued and boundless progression. The only notion we have of it is from the addition or division of finite things, which suggest the idea of infinite, only from a power we feel in ourselves of still multiplying and dividing without end. The Schoolmen indeed were bolder, and, by a summary mode of reasoning, in which they were very expert, proved that they had as clear and adequate an idea of infinity, as of any finite substance whatever. Infinity, said they, is that which has no bounds. This negation, being a positive assertion, must be founded on a positive idea. We have therefore a positive idea of infinity.

The Eclectic Jews, and their followers, the Ammonian and Christian Platonics, who endeavoured to make their own philosophy and religion conform to the ancient theology, held infinity of space to be only the immensity of the divine presence. ʽΟ Θεος ἑαντσ τοπος εστι [1] was their dogma, which is now inserted into the Confessional of the Greek Church.[2] This infinity was distinguished by them from common space, as time was from eternity. Whatever is eternal or infinite, said they, must be absolutely indivisible; because division is in itself inconsistent with

[1] Philo. *de Leg. Alleg.* lib. 1. Jo Damasc *de Orth Fid.*
[2] Mosheim. Nota in Sec. xxiv. Cudw. *Syst. Intellect.*

46

infinite continuity and duration: therefore space and time are distinct from infinity and eternity, which are void of all parts and gradations whatever. Time is measured by years, days, hours, &c., and distinguished by past, present, and future; but these, being divisions, are excluded from eternity, as locality is from infinity, and as both are from the Being who fills both; who can therefore feel no succession of events, nor know any gradation of distance; but must comprehend infinite duration as if it were one moment, and infinite extent as if it were but a single point.[1] Hence the Ammonian Platonics speak of him as concentered in his own unity, and extended through all things, but participated of by none. Being of a nature more refined and elevated than intelligence itself, he could not be known by sense, perception, or reason; and being the cause of all, he must be anterior to all, even to eternity itself, if considered as eternity of time, and not as the intellectual unity, which is the Deity himself, by whose emanations all things exist, and to whose proximity or distances they owe their degrees of excellence or baseness. *Being* itself, in its most abstract sense, is derived from him; for that which is the cause and beginning of all *Being*, cannot be a part of that *All* which

[1] See Boeth. *de Consol. Philos.* lib. iv. prof. 6.

47

sprung from himself: therefore he is not *Being*, nor is *Being* his *Attribute;* for that which has an attribute cannot have the abstract simplicity of pure unity. All *Being* is in its nature finite; for, if it was otherwise, it must be without bounds every way; and therefore could have no gradation of proximity to the first cause, or consequent pre-eminence of one part over another: for, as all distinctions of time are excluded from infinite duration, and all divisions of locality from infinite extent, so are all degrees of priority from infinite progression. The mind *is* and *acts* in itself; but the abstract unity of the first cause is neither in itself, nor in another;—not in itself, because that would imply modification, from which abstract simplicity is necessarily exempt; nor in another, because then there would be an hypostatical duality, instead of absolute unity. In both cases there would be a locality of hypostasis, inconsistent with intellectual infinity. As all physical attributes were excluded from this metaphysical abstraction, which they called their first cause, he must of course be destitute of all moral ones, which are only generalized modes of action of the former. Even simple abstract truth was denied him; for truth, as Proclus says, is merely the relative to falsehood; and no relative can exist without a positive or correlative. The

Deity therefore who has no falsehood, can have no truth, in our sense of the word.[1]

As metaphysical theology is a study very generally, and very deservedly, neglected at present, I thought this little specimen of it might be entertaining, from its novelty, to most readers; especially as it is intimately connected with the ancient system, which I have here undertaken to examine. Those, who wish to know more of it, may consult Proclus on the Theology of Plato, where they will find the most exquisite ingenuity most wantonly wasted. No persons ever showed greater acuteness or strength of reasoning than the Platonics and Scholastics; but having quitted common sense, and attempted to mount into the intellectual world, they expended it all in abortive efforts which may amuse the imagination, but cannot satisfy the understanding.

The ancient Theologists showed more discretion; for, finding that they could conceive no idea of infinity, they were content to revere the Infinite Being in the most general and efficient exertion of his power, attraction; whose agency is perceptible through all matter, and to which all motion may, perhaps, be ultimately traced. This power, being personified, became the secondary Deity, to whom all

[1] Proclus *in Theolog. Platon.* lib. i. et ii.

adoration and worship were directed, and who is therefore frequently considered as the sole and supreme cause of all things. His agency being supposed to extend through the whole material world, and to produce all the various revolutions by which its system is sustained, his attributes were of course extremely numerous and varied. These were expressed by various titles and epithets in the mystic hymns and litanies, which the artists endeavoured to represent by various forms and characters of men and animals. The great characteristic attribute was represented by the organ of generation in that state of tension and rigidity which is necessary to the due performance of its functions. Many small images of this kind have been found among the ruins of Herculaneum and Pompeii, attached to the bracelets, which the chaste and pious matrons of antiquity wore round their necks and arms. In these, the organ of generation appears alone, or only accompanied with the wings of incubation,[1] in order to show that the devout wearer devoted herself wholly and solely to procreation, the great end for which she was ordained. So expressive a symbol, being constantly in her view, must keep her attention fixed on its natural object, and continually remind her of the gratitude she owed

[1] Plate II. Fig. 2, engraved from one in the British Museum.

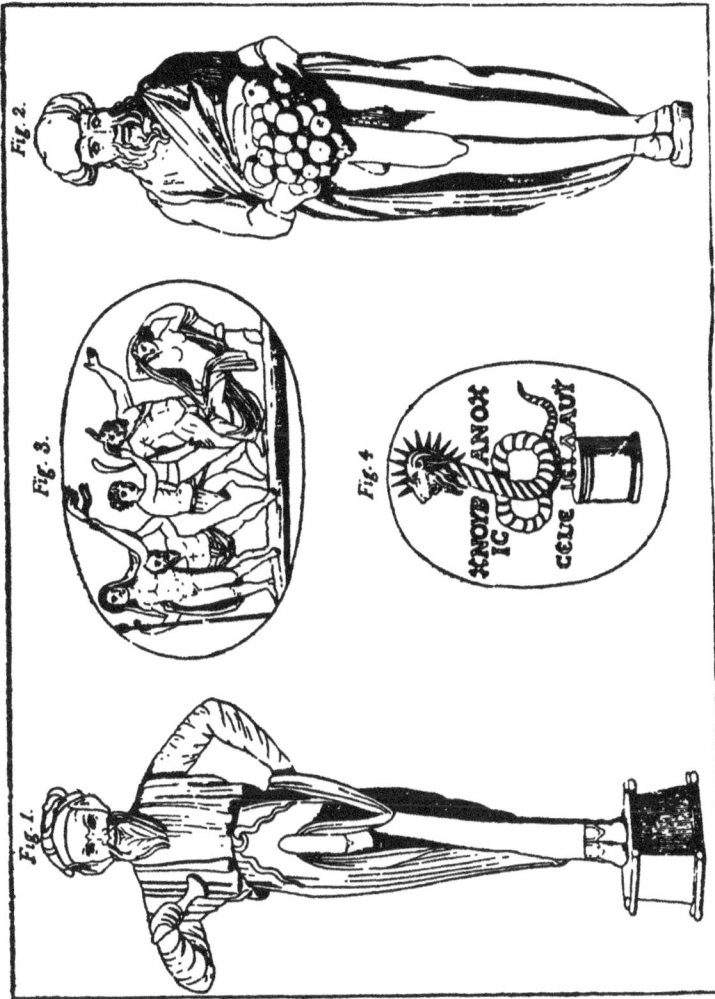

PLATE V

FIGURES OF PAN AND GEMS

the Creator, for having taken her into his service, made her a partaker of his most valuable blessings, and employed her as the passive instrument in the exertion of his most beneficial power.

The female organs of generation were revered [1] as symbols of the generative powers of nature or matter, as the male were of the generative powers of God. They are usually represented emblematically, by the Shell, or *Concha Veneris,* which was therefore worn by devout persons of antiquity, as it still continues to be by pilgrims, and many of the common women of Italy. The union of both was expressed by the hand mentioned in Sir William Hamilton's letter; [2] which being a less explicit symbol, has escaped the attention of the reformers, and is still worn, as well as the shell, by the women of Italy, though without being understood. It represented the act of generation, which was considered as a solemn sacrament, in honour of the Creator, as will be more fully shown hereafter.

The male organs of generation are sometimes found represented by signs of the same sort, which might properly be called the symbols of symbols. One of the most remarkable of these is a cross,

[1] August. *de Civ. Dei*, Lib. vi. c. 9.
[2] See Plate ii, Fig. 1. from one in the British Museum, in which both symbols are united.

in the form of the letter T,[1] which thus served as the emblem of creation and generation, before the church adopted it as the sign of salvation; a lucky coincidence of ideas, which, without doubt, facilitated the reception of it among the faithful. To the representative of the male organs was sometimes added a human head, which gives it the exact appearance of a crucifix; as it has on a medal of Cyzicus, published by M. Pellerin.[2] On an ancient medal, found in Cyprus, which, from the style of workmanship, is certainly anterior to the Macedonian conquest, it appears with the chaplet or rosary, such as is now used in the Romish churches;[3] the beads of which were used, anciently, to reckon time.[4] Their being placed in a circle, marked its progressive continuity; while their separation from each other marked the divisions, by which it is made to return on itself, and thus produce years, months, and days. The symbol of the creative power is placed upon them, because these divisions were particularly under his influence and protection; the sun being his visible image, and the centre of his power, from which his emanations

[1] Recherches sur les Arts, lib. 1. c. 3.

[2] See Plate IX. Fig. 1.

[3] Plate IX. Fig. 2, from Pellerin. Similar medals are in the Hunter Collection, and are evidently of Phœnician work.

[4] Recherches sur les Arts, lib. 1. c. 3.

extended through the universe. Hence the Egyptians, in their sacred hymns, called upon Osiris, as the being who dwelt concealed in the embraces of the sun;[1] and hence the great luminary itself is called Κοσμοχρατωξ (Ruler of the World) in the Orphic Hymns.[2]

This general emanation of the pervading Spirit of God, by which all things are generated and maintained, is beautifully described by Virgil, in the following lines:

> Deum namque ire per omnes
> Terrasque, tractusque maris, cœlumque profundum.
> Hinc pecudes, armenta, viros, genus omne ferarum,
> Quemque sibi tenues nascentum arcessere vitas.
> Scilicet huc reddi deinde, ac resoluta referri
> Omnia: nec morti esse locum, sed viva volare
> Sideris in numerum, atque alto succedere cœlo.[3]

The Ethereal Spirit is here described as expanding itself through the universe, and giving life and motion to the inhabitants of earth, water, and air, by a participation of its own essence, each particle of which returned to its native source, at the dissolution of the body which it animated. Hence, not only men, but all animals, and even vegetables, were supposed to be impregnated with some particles of the

1 Plutarch. *de Is. et Osir.*
2 See Hymn VII.
3 Georgic. lib. iv. ver. 221.

Divine Nature infused into them, from which their various qualities and dispositions, as well as their powers of propagation, were supposed to be derived. These appeared to be so many emanations of the Divine attributes, operating in different modes and degrees, according to the nature of the beings to which they belonged. Hence the characteristic properties of animals and plants were not only regarded as representations, but as actual emanations of the Divine Power, consubstantial with his own essence.[1] For this reason, the symbols were treated with greater respect and veneration than if they had been merely signs and characters of convention. Plutarch says, that most of the Egyptian priests held the bull Apis, who was worshipped with so much ceremony, to be only an image of the Spirit of Osiris.[2] This I take to have been the real meaning of all the animal worship of the Egyptians, about which so much has been written, and so little discovered. Those animals or plants, in which any particular attribute of the Deity seemed to predominate, became the symbols of that attribute, and were accordingly worshipped as the images of Divine Providence, acting in that particular direction. Like many

[1] Proclus *in Theol. Plat.* lib. 1. pp. 56, 57.
[2] *De Is. et Os.*

PLATE VI

THE TAURIC DIANA

other customs, both of ancient and modern worship, the practice, probably, continued long after the reasons upon which it was founded were either wholly lost, or only partially preserved, in vague traditions. This was the case in Egypt; for, though many of the priests knew or conjectured the origin of the worship of the bull, they could give no rational account why the crocodile, the ichneumon, and the ibis, received similar honours. The symbolical characters, called hieroglyphics, continued to be esteemed by them as more holy and venerable than the conventional representations of sounds, notwithstanding their manifest inferiority; yet it does not appear, from any accounts extant, that they were able to assign any reason for this preference. On the contrary, Strabo tells us that the Egyptians of his time were wholly ignorant of their ancient learning and religion,[1] though impostors continually pretended to explain it. Their ignorance in these points is not to be wondered at, considering that the most ancient Egyptians, of whom we have any authentic accounts, lived after the subversion of their monarchy and destruction of their temples by the Persians, who used every endeavour to annihilate their religion; first, by command of Cambyses,[2] and then of Ochus.[3] What they

[1] Lib. xvii.   [2] Herodot. lib. iii.   Strabo, lib. xvii.
[3] Plutarch. *de Is. et Os.*

were before this calamity, we have no direct information; for Herodotus is the earliest traveller, and he visited this country when in ruins.

It is observable in all modern religions, that men are superstitious in proportion as they are ignorant, and that those who know least of the principles of religion are the most earnest and fervent in the practice of its exterior rites and ceremonies. We may suppose from analogy, that this was the case with the Egyptians. The learned and rational merely respected and revered the sacred animals, whilst the vulgar worshipped and adored them. The greatest part of the former being, as is natural to suppose, destroyed by the persecution of the Persians, this worship and adoration became general; different cities adopting different animals as their tutelar deities, in the same manner as the Catholics now put themselves under the protection of different saints and martyrs. Like them, too, in the fervency of their devotion for the imaginary agent, they forgot the original cause.

The custom of keeping sacred animals as images of the Divine attributes, seems once to have prevailed in Greece as well as Egypt; for the God of Health was represented by a living serpent at Epidaurus, even in the last stage of their religion. [1] In

[1] Liv. *Hist. Epitom.* lib. xi.

general, however, they preferred wrought images, not from their superiority in art, which they did not acquire until after the time of Homer,[1] when their theology was entirely corrupted; but because they had thus the means of expressing their ideas more fully, by combining several forms together, and showing, not only the Divine attribute, but the mode and purpose of its operation. For instance; the celebrated bronze in the Vatican has the male organs of generation placed upon the head of a cock, the emblem of the sun, supported by the neck and shoulders of a man. In this composition they represented the generative power of the Ερως, the Osiris, Mithras, or Bacchus, whose centre is the sun, incarnate with man. By the inscription on the pedestal, the attribute this personified, is styled *The Saviour of the World* (Σωτηζ κοσμψ); a title always venerable, under whatever image it be represented.[2]

The Egyptians showed this incarnation of the Deity by a less permanent, though equally expressive symbol. At Mendes a living goat was kept as the image of the generative power, to whom the women presented themselves naked, and had the honour of being publicly enjoyed by him. Herodotus saw the act

[1] When Homer praises any work of art, he calls it the work of Sidonians.
[2] See Plate II. Fig. 3.

openly performed (ες επιδειξιν ανθρωπων), and calls it a prodigy (τερας). But the Egyptians had no such horror of it; for it was to them a representation of the incarnation of the Deity, and the communication of his creative spirit to man. It was one of the sacraments of that ancient church, and was, without doubt, beheld with that pious awe and reverence with which devout persons always contemplate the mysteries of their faith, whatever they happen to be; for, as the learned and orthodox Bishop Warburton, whose authority it is not for me to dispute, says, *from the nature of any action morality cannot arise, nor from its effects;* [1] therefore, for aught we can tell, this ceremony, however shocking it may appear to modern manners and opinions, might have been intrinsically meritorious at the time of its celebration, and afforded a truly edifying spectacle to the saints of ancient Egypt. Indeed, the Greeks do not seem to have felt much horror or disgust at the imitative representation of it, whatever the historian might have thought proper to express at the real celebration. Several specimens of their sculpture in this way have escaped the fury of the reformers, and remained for the instruction of later times. One of these, found among the ruins of Herculaneum, and

[1] Div. Leg. book 1. c. 4.

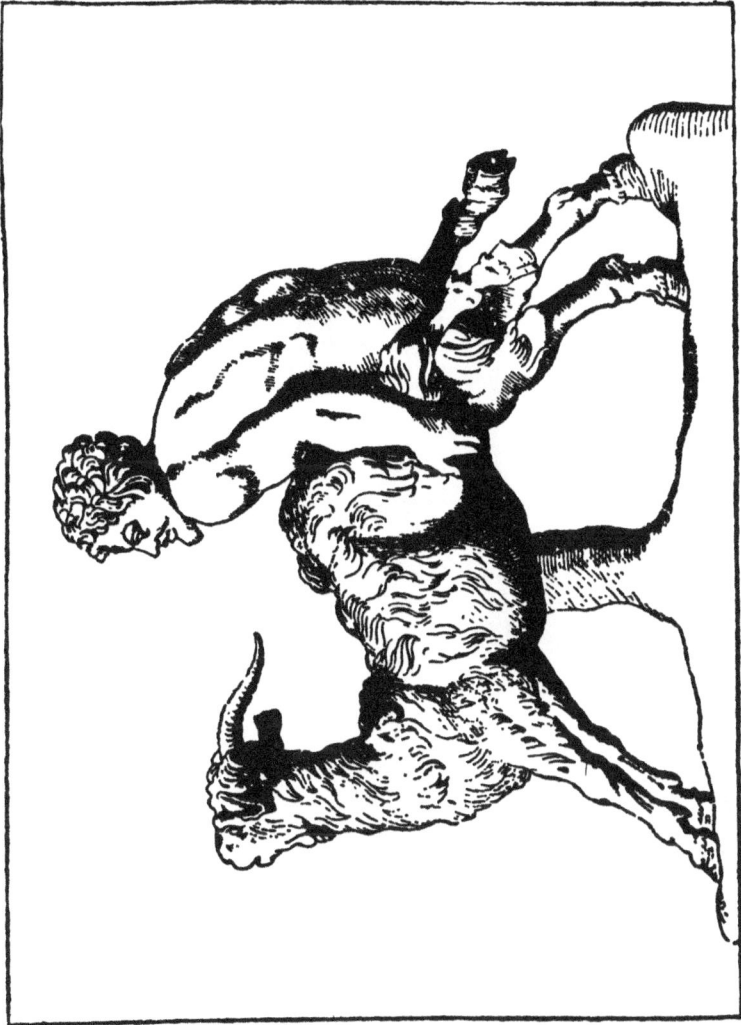

PLATE VII

GOAT AND SATYR. GREEK SCULPTURE

kept concealed in the Royal Museum of Portici, is well known. Another exists in the collection of Mr. Townley, which I have thought proper to have engraved for the benefit of the learned.[1] It may be remarked, that in these monuments the goat is *passive* instead of *active;* and that the *human symbol* is represented as incarnate with the *divine,* instead of the *divine* with the *human:* but this is in fact no difference; for the Creator, being of both sexes, is represented indifferently of either. In the other symbol of the bull, the sex is equally varied; the Greek medals having sometimes a bull, and sometimes a cow,[2] which, Strabo tells us, was employed as the symbol of Venus, the passive generative power, at Momemphis, in Egypt.[3] Both the bull and the cow are also worshipped at present by the Hindoos, as symbols of the male and female, or generative and nutritive, powers of the Deity. The cow is in almost all their pagodas; but the bull is revered with superior solemnity and devotion. At Tanjour is a monument of their piety to him, which even the inflexible perseverance, and habitual industry of the natives of that country, could scarcely have erected

[1] See Plate vii.

[2] See Plate iv. Fig. 1, 2, 3, and Plate iii. Fig. 4, engraved from medals belonging to me.

[3] Lib. xvii.

without greater knowledge in practical mechanics than they now possess. It is a statue of a bull lying down, hewn, with great accuracy, out of a single piece of hard granite, which has been conveyed by land from the distance of one hundred miles, although its weight, in its present reduced state, must be at least one hundred tons.[1] The Greeks sometimes made their Taurine Bacchus, or bull, with a human face, to express both sexes, which they signified by the initial of the epithet Διφνης placed under him.[2] Over him they frequently put the radiated asterisk, which represents the sun, to show the Deity, whose attribute he was intended to express.[3] Hence we may perceive the reason why the Germans, who, according to Cæsar,[4] worshipped the sun, carried a brazen bull, as the image of their God, when they invaded the Roman dominions in the time of Marius;[5] and even the chosen people of Providence, when they made unto themselves an image of the God who was to conduct them through the desert,

[1] See Plate xxII. with the measurements, as made by Capt. Patterson on the spot.

[2] See Plate IV. Fig. 2, from a medal of Naples in the Hunter collection.

[3] See Plate IV. Fig. 2, and Plate xIX. Fig. 4, from a medal of Cales, belonging to me.

[4] *De B. G.*, lib. vi.

[5] Plut. *in Mario.*

and cast out the ungodly, from before them, made it in the shape of a young bull, or calf.[1]

The Greeks, as they advanced in the cultivation of the imitative arts, gradually changed the animal for the human form, preserving still the original character. The human head was at first added to the body of the bull;[2] but afterwards the whole figure was made human, with some of the features, and general character of the animal, blended with it.[3] Oftentimes, however, these mixed figures had a peculiar and proper meaning, like that of the Vatican Bronze; and were not intended as mere refinements of art. Such are the fawns and satyrs, who represent the emanations of the Creator, incarnate with man, acting as his angels and ministers in the work of universal generation. In copulation with the goat, they represent the reciprocal incarnation of man with the deity, when incorporated with universal matter: for the Deity, being both male and female, was both active and passive in procreation; first animating man by an emanation from his own essence, and then employing that emanation to reproduce, in conjunction with the common productive powers of nature,

[1] *Exod.* c. xxxii., with Patrick's *Commentary*.

[2] See the medals of Naples, Gela &c. Plate iv. Fig. 2. and Plate ix. Fig. ii, are specimens; but the coins are in all collections.

[3] See *Bronzi d'Herculano*, tom. v. Plate v.

which are no other than his own prolific spirit transfused through matter.

These mixed beings are derived from Pan, the principle of universal order; of whose personified image they partake. Pan is addressed in the Orphic Litanies as the first-begotten love, or creator incorporated in universal matter, and so forming the world.[1] The heaven, the earth, water, and fire are said to be members of him; and he is described as the origin and source of all things (παντοφυης γενετωζπατων), as representing matter animated by the Divine Spirit. Lycæan Pan was the most ancient and revered God of the Arcadians,[2] the most ancient people of Greece. The epithet Lycæan (Λνκαοις), is usually derived from λνκος, a wolf; though it is impossible to find any relation which this etymology can have with the deities to which it is applied; for the epithet Λνκαιος, or Λνκειος (which is only the different pronunciation of a different dialect), is occasionally applied to almost all the gods. I have therefore no doubt, but that it ought to be derived from the old word λνκος, or λνκη, light; from which came the Latin word *lux*.[3] In this sense it is a very proper epithet for the Divine Nature, of whose essence light was supposed

[1] Hymn. x.
[2] Dionys. *Antiq. Rom.* lib. i. c. 32.
[3] Macrob. *Sat.* xvii.

PLATE VIII

BRONZE STATUE OF CERES

to be. I am confirmed in this conjecture by a word
in the *Electra* of Sophocles, which seems hitherto to
have been misunderstood. At the opening of the
play, the old tutor of Orestes, entering Argos with
his young pupil, points out to him the most celebrated
public buildings, and amongst them the Lycæan Fo-
rum, τψ λνκοκτονψ Θεψ, which the scholiast and translators interpret, *of the wolf-killing God*, though
there is no reason whatever why this epithet should
be applied to Apollo. But, if we derive the compound
from λνκος, light, and εκτεινειν, to extend, instead of
κτεινειν, to kill, the meaning will be perfectly just
and natural; for *light-extending*, is of all others the
properest epithet for the sun. Sophocles, as well as
Virgil, is known to have been an admirer of ancient
expressions, and to have imitated Homer more than
any other Attic Poet; therefore, his employing an obsolete word is not to be wondered at. Taking this
etymology as the true one, the Lycæan Pan of Ar-
cadia is Pan *the luminous;* that is, the divine essence
of light incorporated in universal matter. The Arcadians called him τον της νλης Κνριον, the lord of matter as Macrobius rightly translates it.[1] He was hence
called Sylvanus by the Latins; *Sylvus* being, in the
ancient Pelasgian and Æolian Greek, from which the

[1] Sat. 1. c. 22.

Latin is derived, the same as ὕλη; for it is well known to all who have compared the two languages attentively, that the *Sigma* and *Vau* are letters, the one of which was partially, and the other generally omitted by the Greeks, in the refinement of their pronunciation and orthography which took place after the emigration of the Latian and Etruscan colonies. The Chorus in the *Ajax* of Sophocles address Pan by the title of ʽΑλιπλαγκτος,[1] probably because he was worshipped on the shores of the sea; water being reckoned the best and most prolific of the subordinate elements,[2] upon which the Spirit of God, according to Moses, or the Plastic Nature, according to the Platonics, operating, produced life and motion on earth. Hence the ocean is said by Homer to be the source of all things;[3] and hence the use of water in baptism, which was to regenerate, and, in a manner, new create the person baptised; for the soul, supposed by many of the primitive Christians to be naturally mortal, was then supposed to become immortal.[4] Upon the same principle, the figure of Pan,[5]

[1] Ver. 703.

[2] Pindar. *Olymp.* i. ver i. Diodor. Sic. lib. i. p. ii.

[3] Il. Θ, ver. 246, and ζ, ver. 196.

[4] Clementina, *Hom.* xii. Arnob. *adv.* Gentes, lib. ii.

[5] See Plate v. Fig. i. The original is among the antiquities found in Herculaneum, now in the Museum of Portici.

is represented pouring water upon the organ of generation; that is, invigorating the active creative power
by the prolific element upon which it acted; for water
was considered as the essence of the passive principle, as fire was of the active; the one being of terrestrial, and the other of æthereal origin. Hence, St.
John the Baptist, who might have acquired some
knowledge of the ancient theology, through its re-
vivers, the Eclectic Jews, says: *I, indeed, baptise you
in water to repentance; but he that cometh after me,
who is more powerful than I am, shall baptise you in
the Holy Spirit, and in fire:* [1] that is, I only purify
and refresh the soul, by a communion with the terrestrial principle of life; but he that cometh after me,
will regenerate and restore it, by a communion with
the æthereal principle. [2] Pan is again addressed in
the Salaminian Chorus of the same tragedy of Sophocles, by the titles of author and director of the dances
of the gods (Θεων χοροποι' αναξ), as being the author
and disposer of the regular motions of the universe,
of which these divine dances were symbols, which
are said in the same passage to be (αντοδαη) *self-*

[1] *Matth.* c. iii.

[2] It is the avowed intention of the learned and excellent work
of Grotius, to prove that there is nothing new in Christianity.
What I have here adduced, may serve to confirm and illustrate
the discoveries of that great and good man. *See de Veritate
Relig. Christ.* lib. iv, c. 12.

taught to him. Both the Gnossian and Nysian dances are here included,[1] the former sacred to Jupiter, and the latter to Bacchus; for Pan, being the principle of universal order, partook of the nature of all the other gods. They were personifications of particular modes of acting of the great all-ruling principle; and he, of his general law and pre-established harmony by which he governs the universe. Hence he is often represented playing on a pipe; music being the natural emblem of this physical harmony. According to Plutarch, the Jupiter Ammon of the Africans was the same as the Pan of the Greeks.[2] This explains the reason why the Macedonian kings assumed the horns of that god; for, though Alexander pretended to be his son, his successors never pretended to any such honour; and yet they equally assumed the symbols, as appears from their medals.[3] The case is, that Pan, or Ammon, being the universe, and Jupiter a title of the Supreme God (as will be shown hereafter), the horns, the emblems of his power, seemed the properest symbols of that supreme and universal dominion to which they all, as well as Alexander,

[1] Ver. 708.

[2] *De Is. et Os.*

[3] See Plate IV. Fig 4, engraved from one of Lysimachus, of exquisite beauty, belonging to me. Antigonus put the head of Pan upon his coins, which are not uncommon.

had the ambition to aspire. The figure of Ammon was compounded of the forms of the ram, as that of Pan was of the goat; the reason of which is difficult to ascertain, unless we suppose that goats were unknown in the country where his worship arose, and that the ram expressed the same attribute.[1] In a gem in the Museum of Charles Townley, Esq., the head of the Greek Pan is joined to that of a ram, on the body of a cock, over whose head is the asterisk of the sun, and below it the head of an aquatic fowl, attached to the same body.[2] The cock is the symbol of the sun, probably from proclaiming his approach in the morning; and the aquatic fowl is the emblem of water; so that this composition, apparently so whimsical, represents the universe between the two great prolific elements, the one the active, and the other the passive cause of all things.

The Creator being both male and female, the emanations of his creative spirit, operating upon universal matter, produced subordinate ministers of both sexes, and gave, as companions to the fauns and satyrs, the nymphs of the waters, the mountains and the woods, signifying the passive productive powers

[1] Pausanias (lib. ii.) says he knew the meaning of this symbol, but did not choose to reveal it, it being a part of the mystic worship.

[2] Plate III. Fig. I.

of each, subdivided and diffused. Of the same class are the Γενετυλλιδες, mentioned by Pausanias as companions to Venus,[1] who, as well as Ceres, Juno, Diana, Isis, &c., was only a personification of nature, or the passive principle of generation, operating in various modes. Apuleius invokes Isis by the names of the Eleusinian Ceres, Celestial Venus, and Proserpine; and, when the Goddess answers him, she describes herself as follows: "I am," says she, "nature, the parent of things, the sovereign of the elements, the primary progeny of time, the most exalted of the deities, the first of the heavenly Gods and Goddesses, the queen of the shades, the uniform countenance; who dispose, with my nod, the luminous heights of heaven, the salubrious breezes of the sea, and the mournful silence of the dead; whose single Deity the whole world venerates, in many forms, with various rites, and various names. The Egyptians, skilled in ancient learning, worship me with proper ceremonies, and call me by my true name, Queen Isis."[2]

According to the Egyptians, Isis copulated with her brother Osiris in the womb of their mother; from whence sprung Arueris, or Orus, the Apollo of the

[1] Lib. i.

[2] *Metamorph.* lib. xi.

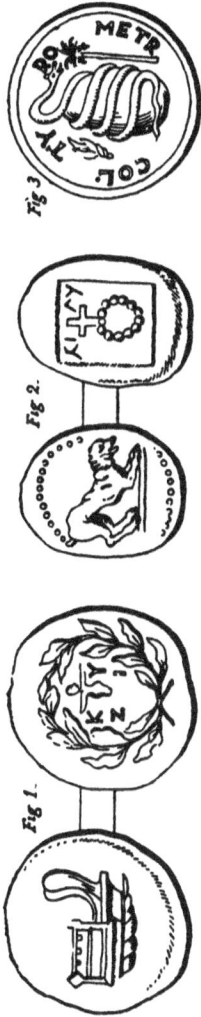

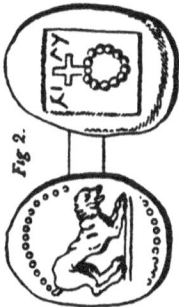

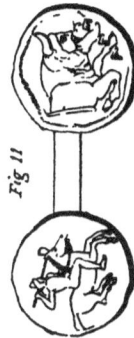

PLATE IX

COINS AND MEDALS

Greeks.[1] This allegory means no more than that the active and passive powers of creation united in the womb of night; where they had been implanted by the unknown father, Κϱονος, or time, and by their union produced the separation or delivery of the elements from each other; for the name Apollo is only a title derived from απολυω, *to deliver from.*[2] They made the robes of Isis various in their colours and complicated in their folds, because the passive or material power appeared in various shapes and modes, as accommodating itself to the active; but the dress of Osiris was simple, and of one luminous colour, to show the unity of his essence, and universality of his power; equally the same through all things.[3] The luminous, or flame colour, represented the sun, who, in the language of the theologists, was the substance of his sacred power, and the visible image of his intellectual being.[4] He is called, in the Orphic Litanies, the chain which connects all things together (ο δ' ανεδϱαμε δεσμος απαντων),[5] as being the principle of attraction; and the deliverer (λνσιος),[6] as giving liberty to the innate powers of

[1] Plutarch, *de Is. et Os.*
[2] Damm. *Lex. Etym.*
[3] Plutarch. *de Is. et Os.*
[4] Ibid.
[5] Hymn. xlvi.
[6] Hymn. xlix. the initials of this epithet are with the bull on

nature, and thus fertilising matter. These epithets not only express the theological, but also the physical system of the Orphic school; according to which the sun, being placed in the centre of the universe, with the planets moving round, was, by his attractive force, the cause of all union and harmony in the whole; and, by the emanation of his beams, the cause of all motion and activity in the parts. This system is alluded to by Homer in the allegory of the golden chain, by which Jupiter suspends all things; [1] though there is every reason to believe that the poet himself was ignorant of its meaning, and only related it as he had heard it. The Ammonian Platonics adopted the same system of attraction, but changed its centre from the sun to their metaphysical abstraction or incomprehensible unity, whose emanations pervaded all things, and held all things together.[2]

Besides the Fauns, Satyrs, and Nymphs, the incarnate emanations of the active and passive powers of the Creator, we often find in the ancient sculptures

a medal of Naples belonging to me The bull has a human countenance, and has therefore been called a minotaur by antiquarians; notwithstanding he is to be fcund on different medals, accompanied with all the symbols both of Bacchus and Apollo, and with the initials of most of the epithets to be found in the Orphic Litanies.

[1] Il. ϴ, ver. xix.

[2] Proclus *in Theol. Plat.* lib. i. c. 21.

certain androgynous beings possessed of the characteristic organs of both sexes, which I take to represent organized matter in its first stage; that is, immediately after it was released from chaos, and
before it was animated by a participation of the
ethereal essence of the Creator. In a beautiful gem
belonging to R. Wilbraham, Esq.,[1] one of these androgynous figures is represented sleeping, with the
organs of generation covered, and the egg of chaos
broken under it. On the other side is Bacchus, the
Creator, bearing a torch, the emblem of ethereal fire,
and extending it towards the sleeping figure; whilst
one of his agents seems only to wait his permission
to begin the execution of that office, which, according
to every outward and visible sign, he appears able to
discharge with energy and effect. The Creator himself leans upon one of those figures commonly called
Sileni; but which, from their heavy unwieldy forms,
were probably intended as personifications of brute
inert matter, from which all things are formed, but
which, being incapable of producing anything of
itself, is properly represented as the support of the
creative power, though not actively instrumental in
his work. The total baldness of this figure represents the exhausted, unproductive state of matter,

[1] See Plate v. Fig. 3.

when the generative powers were separated from it; for it was an opinion of the ancients, which I remember to have met with in some part of the works of Aristotle, to which I cannot at present refer, that every act of coition produced a transient chill in the brain, by which some of the roots of the hair were loosened; so that baldness was a mark of sterility acquired by excessive exertion. The figures of Pan have nearly the same forms with that which I have here supposed to represent inert matter; only that they are compounded with those of the goat, the symbol of the creative power, by which matter was fructified and regulated. To this is sometimes added the organ of generation, of an enormous magnitude, to signify the application of this power to its noblest end, the procreation of sensitive and rational beings. This composition forms the common Priapus of the Roman poets, who was worshipped among the other personages of the heathen mythology, but understood by few of his ancient votaries any better than by the good women of Isernia. His characteristic organ is sometimes represented by the artists in that state of tension and rigidity, which it assumes when about to discharge its functions,[1] and at other times in that state of tumid languor, which immediately

1 Plate v. Fig. 1, from a bronze in the Museum at Portici.

succeeds the performance.[1] In the latter case he appears loaded with the productions of nature, the result of those prolific efforts, which in the former case he appeared so well qualified to exert. I have in Plate v. given a figure of him in each situation, one taken from a bronze in the Royal Museum of Portici, and the other from one in that of Charles Townley, Esq. It may be observed, that in the former the muscles of the face are all strained and contracted, so that every nerve seems to be in a state of tension; whereas in the latter the features are all dilated and fallen, the chin reposed on the breast, and the whole figure expressive of languor and fatigue.

If the explanation which I have given of these androgynous figures be the true one, the fauns and satyrs, which usually accompany them, must represent abstract emanations, and not incarnations of the creative spirit, as when in copulation with the goat. The Creator himself is frequently represented in a human form; and it is natural that his emanations should partake of the same, though without having any thing really human in their composition. It seems, however, to have been the opinion in some parts of Asia, that the Creator was really of a human form. The Jewish legislator says expressly, that God

[1] Plate v. Fig 2, from a bronze in the Museum of C. Townley, Esq.

made man in his own image, and, prior to the creation of woman, created him *male and female,*[1] as he himself consequently was.[2] Hence an ingenious author has supposed that these androgynous figures represented the first individuals of the human race, who, possessing the organs of both sexes, produced children of each. This seems to be the sense in which they were represented by some of the ancient artists; but I have never met with any trace of it in any Greek author, except Philo the Jew; nor have I ever seen any monument of ancient art, in which the Bacchus, or Creator in a human form, was represented with the generative organs of both sexes. In the symbolical images, the double nature is frequently expressed by some androgynous insect, such as the snail, which is endowed with the organs of both sexes, and can copulate reciprocally with either: but when the refinement of art adopted the human form, it was represented by mixing the characters of the male and female bodies in every part, preserving still the distinctive organs of the male. Hence Euripides calls Bacchus θηλυμορφος,[3] and the Chorus of Bachannals in the same tragedy address him by masculine and

[1] Genes. c. 1.
[2] Philo. *de. Leg. Alleg.* lib. ii.
[3] Bach. v. 358.

feminine epithets.[1] Ovid also says to him,

——Tibi, cum sine cornibus adstas,
Virgineum caput est.[2]

alluding in the first line to his taurine, and in the
second to his androgynous figure.

The ancient theologists were, like the modern, divided into sects; but, as these never disturbed the
peace of society, they have been very little noticed. I
have followed what I conceive to be the true Orphic
system, in the little analysis which I have here endeavoured to give. This was probably the true catholic faith, though it differs considerably from another
ancient system, described by Aristophanes; [3] which is
more poetical, but less philosophical. According to
this, Chaos, Night, Erebus, and Tartarus, were the
primitive beings. Night, in the infinite breast of
Erebus, brought forth an egg, from which sprung
Love, who mixed all things together; and from thence
sprung the heaven, the ocean, the earth, and the gods.
This system is alluded to by the epithet Ωογενος, applied to the Creator in one of the Orphic Litanies: [4]
but this could never have been a part of the orthodox

[1] Ω Βρομιε, Βρομιε, Πεδωνρθσνος ενοσι ποτνια. Vers. 504.
[2] *Metam.* lib. iv. v. 18.
[3] Ορνιθ. Vers. 693.
[4] Hymn v.

faith; for the Creator is usually represented as breaking the egg of chaos, and therefore could not have sprung from it. In the confused medleys of allegories and traditions contained in the Theogony attributed to Hesiod, Love is placed after Chaos and the Earth, but anterior to every thing else. These differences are not to be wondered at; for Aristophanes, supposing that he understood the true system, could not with safety have revealed it, or even mentioned it any otherwise than under the usual garb of fiction and allegory; and as for the author of the Theogony, it is evident, from the strange jumble of incoherent fables which he has put together, that he knew very little of it. The system alluded to in the Orphic verses quoted in the *Argonautics,* is in all probability the true one; for it is not only consistent in all its parts, but contains a physical truth, which the greatest of the modern discoveries has only confirmed and explained. The others seem to have been only poetical corruptions of it, which, extending by degrees, produced that unwieldly system of poetical mythology, which constituted the vulgar religion of Greece.

The fauns and satyrs, which accompany the androgynous figures on the ancient sculptures, are usually represented as ministering to the Creator by exerting their characteristic attributes upon them, as well as upon the nymphs, the passive agents of pro-

PLATE X.

Fig. 1.

Fig. 8.

Fig. 2.

Fig. 6.

Fig. 4.

Fig. 7.

Fig. 3.

Fig. 5.

PLATE X

SYSTRUM, WITH VARIOUS MEDALS

creation: but what has puzzled the learned in these monuments, and seems a contradiction to the general system of ancient religion, is that many of these groups are in attitudes which are rather adapted to the gratification of disordered and unnatural appetites, than to extend procreation. But a learned author, who has thrown infinite light upon these subjects, has effectually cleared them from this suspicion, by showing that they only took the most convenient way to get at the female organs of generation, in those mixed beings who possessed both.[1] This is confirmed by Lucretius, who asserts, that this attitude is better adapted to the purposes of generation than any other.[2] We may therefore conclude, that instead of representing them in the act of gratifying any disorderly appetites, the artists meant to show their modesty in not indulging their concupiscence, but in doing their duty in the way best adapted to answer the ends proposed by the Creator.

On the Greek medals, where the cow is the symbol of the deity, she is frequently represented licking a calf, which is sucking her.[3] This is probably meant to show that the creative power cherishes and nour-

---

[1] *Recherches sur les Arts,* iv. i. c. 3.

[2] Lib. iv. v. 1260.

[3] See Plate iv. Fig. 3, from a medal of Dyrrachium, belonging to me.

ishes, as well as generates; for, as all quadrupeds lick their young, to refresh and invigorate them immediately after birth, it is natural to suppose, according to the general system of symbolical writing, that this action should be taken as an emblem of the effect it was thought to produce. On other medals the bull or cow is represented licking itself;[1] which, upon the same principle, must represent the strength of the deity refreshed and invigorated by the exertion of its own nutritive and plastic power upon its own being. On others again is a human head of an androgynous character, like that of the Bacchus διφνης, with the tongue extended over the lower lip, as if to lick something.[2] This was probably the same symbol, expressed in a less explicit manner; it being the common practice of the Greek artists to make a part of a composition signify the whole, of which I shall soon have occasion to give some incontestable examples. On a Parian medal published by Goltzius, the bull licking himself is represented on one side, accompanied by the asterisk of the sun, and on the other, the head with the tongue extended, having serpents, the emblems of life, for hair.[3] The same medal is in

[1] See Plate III. Fig. 5, from one of Gortyna, in the Hunter Collection; and Plate III. Fig. 4, from one of Parium, belonging to me.

[2] See Plate III. Fig. 4, and Plate III. Fig. 6, from Pellerin.

[3] Goltz. *Insul.* Tab. xix. Fig. 8.

my collection, except that the serpents are not attached to the head, but placed by it as distinct symbols, and that the animal licking itself is a female
accompanied by the initial of the word Θεος, instead of the asterisk of the sun. Antiquarians have
called this head a Medusa; but, had they examined
it attentively on any well-preserved coin, they would
have found that the expression of the features means
lust, and not rage or horror.[1] The case is, that antiquarians have been continually led into error, by
seeking for explanations of the devices on the Greek
medals in the wild and capricious stories of Ovid's
Metamorphoses, instead of examining the first principles of ancient religion contained in the Orphic
Fragments, the writings of Plutarch, Macrobius, and
Apulcius, and the Choral Odes of the Greek tragedies.
These principles were the subjects of the ancient
mysteries, and it is to these that the symbols on the
medals always relate; for they were the public acts
of the states, and therefore contain the sense of
nations, and not the caprices of individuals.

As M. D'Hancarville found a complete representation of the bull breaking the egg of chaos in the sculptures of the Japanese, when only a part of it appears
on the Greek monuments; so we may find in a curi-

[1] See Plate III. Fig. 4.

ous Oriental fragment, lately brought from the sacred caverns of Elephanta, near Bombay, a complete representation of the symbol so enigmatically expressed by the head above mentioned. These caverns are ancient places of worship, hewn in the solid rock with immense labour and difficulty. That from which the fragment in question was brought, is 130 feet long by 110 wide, adorned with columns and sculptures finished in a style very different from that of the Indian artists.[1] It is now neglected; but others of the same kind are still used as places of worship by the Hindoos, who can give no account of the antiquity of them, which must necessarily be very remote, for the Hindoos are a very ancient people; and yet the sculptures represent a race of men very unlike them, or any of the present inhabitants of India. A specimen of these was brought from the island of Elephanta, in the Cumberland man-of-war, and now belongs to the museum of Mr. Townley. It contains several figures, in very high relief; the principal of which are a man and woman, in an attitude which I shall not venture to describe, but only observe, that the action, which I have supposed to be a symbol of refreshment and invigoration, is mutually applied by both to their respective organs of genera-

[1] *Archoel.* vol. viii. p. 289.

tion,[1] the emblems of the active and passive powers of procreation, which mutually cherish and invigorate each other.

The Hindoos still represent the creative powers of the deity by these ancient symbols, the male and female organs of generation; and worship them with the same pious reverence as the Greeks and Egyptians did.[2] Like them too they have buried the original principles of their theology under a mass of poetical mythology, so that few of them can give any more perfect account of their faith, than that they mean to worship one first cause, to whom the subordinate deities are merely agents, or more properly personified modes of action.[3] This is the doctrine inculcated, and very fully explained, in the *Bagvat Geeta;* a moral and metaphysical work lately translated from the Sanscrit language, and said to have been written upwards of four thousand years ago. Kreshna, or the deity become incarnate in the shape of man, in order to instruct all mankind, is introduced, revealing to his disciples the fundamental principles of true faith, religion, and wisdom; which are the exact counterpart of the system of emanations, so beautifully described in the lines of

[1] See Plate xi.
[2] Sonnerat, *Voyage aux Ines.* T. 1. p. 180.
[3] Niebuhr, *Voyages*, vol. II. p. 17.

Virgil before cited. We here find, though in a more mystic garb, the same one principle of life universally emanated and expanded, and ever partially returning to be again absorbed in the infinite abyss of intellectual being. This reabsorption, which is throughout recommended as the ultimate end of human perfection, can only be obtained by a life of inward meditation and abstract thought, too steady to be interrupted by any worldly incidents, or disturbed by any transitory affections, whether of mind or body. But as such a life is not in the power of any but a Brahman, inferior rewards, consisting of gradual advancements during the transmigrations of the soul, are held out to the soldier, the husbandman, and mechanic, accordingly as they fulfill the duties of their several stations. Even those who serve other gods are not excluded from the benefits awarded to every moral virtue; for, as the divine Teacher says, *If they do it with a firm belief, in so doing they involuntarily worship even me. I am he who partaketh of all worship, and I am their reward.*[1] This universal deity, being the cause of all motion, is alike the cause of creation, preservation, and destruction; which three attributes are all expressed in the mystic syllable *om*. To repeat this in silence, with firm

[1] *Bagvat Geeta*, p. 81.

PLATE XI

SCULPTURE FROM ELEPHANTA

devotion, and immoveable attention, is the surest means of perfection,[1] and consequent reabsorption, since it leads to the contemplation of the Deity, in his three great characteristic attributes.

The first and greatest of these, the creative or generative attribute, seems to have been originally represented by the union of the male and female organs of generation, which, under the title of the *Lingam*, still occupies the central and most interior recesses of their temples or pagodas; and is also worn, attached to bracelets, round their necks and arms.[2] In a little portable temple brought from the Rohilla country during the late war, and now in the British Museum, this composition appears mounted on a pedestal, in the midst of a square area, sunk in a block of white alabaster.[3] Round the pedestal is a serpent, the emblem of life, with his head rested upon his tail, to denote eternity, or the constant return of time upon itself, whilst it flows through perpetual duration, in regular revolutions and stated periods. From under the body of the serpent springs the lotus or water lily, the Nelumbo of Linnæus, which overspreads the whole of the area not occupied by the figures at the corners. This plant grows

[1] Bagvat Geeta p. 74.
[2] Sonnerat, *Voyage aux Indes*, liv. ii. p. 180. Planche. LIV.
[3] See Plate XII.

in the water, and, amongst its broad leaves, puts
forth a flower, in the center of which is formed the
seed-vessel, shaped like a bell or inverted cone, and
punctuated on the top with little cavities or cells, in
which the seeds grow.[1] The orifices of these cells
being too small to let the seeds drop out when ripe,
they shoot forth into new plants, in the places where
they were formed; the bulb of the vessel serving as
a matrice to nourish them, until they acquire such a
degree of magnitude as to burst it open and release
themselves; after which, like other aquatic weeds,
they take root wherever the current deposits them.
This plant therefore, being thus productive of itself,
and vegetating from its own matrice, without being
fostered in the earth, was naturally adopted as the
symbol of the productive power of the waters, upon
which the active spirit of the creator operated in
giving life and vegetation to matter. We accordingly
find it employed in every part of the northern hemisphere, where the symbolical religion, improperly
called idolatry, does or ever did prevail. The sacred
images of the Tartars, Japonese, and Indians, are
almost all placed upon it; of which numerous instances occur in the publications of Kæmpfer, Chappe
D'Auteroche, and Sonnerat. The upper part of the

[1] See Plate xx. Fig. 1.

base of the *Lingam* also consists of this flower, blended and composed with the female organ of generation which it supports: and the ancient author of the *Bagvat Geeta* speaks of the creator Brahma as sitting upon his lotus throne.[1] The figures of Isis, upon the Isiac Table, hold the stem of this plant, surmounted by the seed-vessel in one hand, and the cross,[2] representing the male organs of generation, in the other; thus signifying the universal power, both active and passive, attributed to that goddess. On the same Isiac Table is also the representation of an Egyptian temple, the columns of which are exactly like the plant which Isis holds in her hand, except that the stem is made larger, in order to give it that stability which is necessary to support a roof and entablature.[3] Columns and capitals of the same kind are still existing, in great numbers, among the ruins of Thebes, in Egypt; and more particularly upon those very curious ones in the island of Philæ, on the borders of Ethiopia, which are, probably, the most ancient monuments of art now extant; at least, if we except the neighbouring temples of Thebes. Both were certainly built when that city was the seat of wealth and empire, which it was, even to a

[1] Page 91.
[2] See Plate xviii. Fig. 2, from Pignorius.
[3] See Plate xviii. Fig. 1, from Pignorius.

proverb, during the Trojan war.[1] How long it had then been so, we can form no conjecture; but that it soon after declined, there can be little doubt; for, when the Greeks, in the reign of Psammeticus (generally computed to have been about 530 years after the Siege of Troy), first became personally acquainted with the interior parts of that country, Memphis had been for many ages its capital, and Thebes was in a manner deserted. Homer makes Achilles speak of its immense wealth and grandeur, as a matter generally known and acknowledged; so that it must have been of long established fame, even in that remote age. We may therefore fairly conclude, that the greatest part of the superb edifices now remaining, were executed, or at least begun, before that time; many of them being such as could not have been finished, but in a long term of years, even if we suppose the wealth and power of the ancient kings of Egypt to have equalled that of the greatest of the Roman emperors. The finishing of Trajan's column in three years, has been justly thought a very extraordinary effort; for there must have been, at least, three hundred good sculptors employed upon it: and yet, in the neighbourhood of Thebes, we find whole temples of enormous magnitude, covered with

[1] Hom. *Iliad. i*, ver. 381.

figures carved in the hard and brittle granite of the Libyan mountains, instead of the soft marbles of Paros and Carrara. Travellers, who have visited that country have given us imperfect accounts of the manner in which they are finished; but, if one may judge by those upon the obelisc of Rameses, now lying in fragments at Rome, they are infinitely more laboured than those of Trajan's Column. An eminent sculptor, with whom I examined that obelisc, was decidedly of opinion, that they must have been finished in the manner of gems, with a graving tool; it appearing impossible for a chisel to cut red granite with so much neatness and precision. The age of Rameses is uncertain; but the generality of modern chronologers suppose that he was the same person as Sesostris, and reigned at Thebes about 1500 years before the Christian æra, and about 300 before the Siege of Troy. Their dates are however merely conjectural, when applied to events of this remote antiquity. The Egyptian priests of the Augustan age had a tradition, which they pretended to confirm by records written in hieroglyphics, that their country had once possest the dominion of all Asia and Ethiopia, which their king Ramses, or Rameses, had conquered.[1] Though this account may be exagge-

[1] Tacit, *Ann.* lib. ii. c. 60.

rated, there can be no doubt, from the buildings still remaining, but that they were once at the head of a great empire; for all historians agree that they abhorred navigation, had no sea-port, and never enjoyed the benefits of foreign commerce, without which, Egypt could have no means of acquiring a sufficient quantity of superfluous wealth to erect such expensive monuments, unless from tributary provinces; especially if all the lower part of it was an uncultivated bog, as Herodotus, with great appearance of probability, tells us it anciently was. Yet Homer, who appears to have known all that could be known in his age, and transmitted to posterity all he knew, seems to have heard nothing of their empire or conquests. These were obliterated and forgotten by the rise of new empires; but the renown of their ancient wealth still continued, and afforded a familiar object of comparison, as that of the Mogul does at this day, though he is become one of the poorest sovereigns in the world.

But far as these Egyptian remains lead us into unknown ages, the symbols they contain appear not to have been invented in that country, but to have been copied from those of some other people, still anterior, who dwelt on the other side of the Erythræan ocean. One of the most obvious of them is the hooded snake, which is a reptile peculiar to the

PLATE XII

INDIAN TEMPLE, SHOWING THE LINGAM

south-eastern parts of Asia, but which I found represented, with great accuracy, upon the obelisc of
Rameses, and have also observed frequently repeated
on the Isiac Table, and other symbolical works of
the Egyptians. It is also distinguishable among the
sculptures in the sacred caverns of the island of
Elephanta;[1] and appears frequently added, as a
characteristic symbol, to many of the idols of the
modern Hindoos, whose absurd tales concerning its
meaning are related at length by M. Sonnerat; but
they are not worth repeating. Probably we should
be able to trace the connexion through many more
instances, could we obtain accurate drawings of the
ruins of Upper Egypt.

By comparing the columns which the Egyptians
formed in imitation of the Nelumbo plant, with each
other, and observing their different modes of deco-
rating them, we may discover the origin of that order
of architecture which the Greeks called Corinthian,
from the place of its supposed invention. We first
find the plain bell, or seed-vessel, used as a capital,
without any further alteration than being a little
expanded at bottom, to give it stability.[2] In the next
instance, the same seed-vessel is surrounded by the

[1] Niebuhr, *Voyage*, vol. ii.
[2] See Plate xix. Fig. 6, from Norden.

leaves of some other plant;[1] which is varied in different capitals according to the different meanings intended to be expressed by these additional symbols. The Greeks decorated it in the same manner, with the leaves of the acanthus, and other sorts of foliage; whilst various other symbols of their religion were introduced as ornaments on the entablature, instead of being carved upon the walls of the cell, or shafts of the columns. One of these, which occurs most frequently, is that which the architects call the honey-suckle, but which, as Sir Joseph Banks (to whom I am indebted for all that I have said concerning the Lotus) clearly shewed me, must be meant for the young shoots of this plant, viewed horizontally, just when they have burst the seed-vessel, and are upon the point of falling out of it. The ornament is variously composed on different buildings; it being the practice of the Greeks to make vegetable, as well as animal monsters, by combining different symbolical plants together, and blending them into one; whence they are often extremely difficult to be discovered. But the specimen I have given, is so strongly characterised, that it cannot easily be mistaken.[2] It appears on many Greek medals with the animal symbols and personified attributes of the Deity; which first led me

[1] See Plate xix. Fig. 7, from Norden.
[2] Plate xix. Fig. 3, from the Ionian Antiquities, Ch. ii. Pl. xiii.

to imagine that it was not a mere ornament, but had some mystic meaning, as almost every decoration employed upon their sacred edifices indisputably had.

The square area, over which the Lotus is spread, in the Indian monument before mentioned, was occasionally floated with water; which, by means of a forcing machine, was first thrown in a spout upon the *Lingam*. The pouring of water upon the sacred symbols, is a mode of worship very much practised by the Hindoos, particularly in their devotions to the Bull and the *Lingam*. Its meaning has been already explained, in the instance of the Greek figure of Pan, represented in the act of paying the same kind of worship to the symbol of his own procreative power.[1] The areas of the Greek temples were, in like manner, in some instances, floated with water; of which I shall soon give an example. We also find, not unfrequently, little portable temples, nearly of the same form, and of Greek workmanship: the areas of which were equally floated by means of a fountain in the middle, and which, by the figures in relief that adorn the sides, appear evidently to have been dedicated to the same worship of Priapus, or the *Lingam*.[2] The square area is likewise impressed upon many

[1] See Plate v. Fig. 1.
[2] See Plate xiv. from one in the collection of Mr. Townley.

ancient Greek medals, sometimes divided into four, and sometimes into a greater number of compartments.[1] Antiquarians have supposed this to be merely the impression of something put under the coin, to make it receive the stroke of the die more steadily; but, besides that it is very ill adapted to this purpose, we find many coins which appear, evidently, to have received the stroke of the hammer (for striking with a balance is of late date) on the side marked with this square. But what puts the question out of all doubt, is, that impressions of exactly the same kind are found upon the little Talismans, or mystic pastes, taken out of the Egyptian Mummies, which have no impression whatever on the reverse.[2] On a little brass medal of Syracuse, we also find the asterisc of the Sun placed in the centre of the square, in the same manner as the *Lingam* is on the Indian monument.[3] Why this quadrangular form was adopted, in preference to any other, we have no means of discovering, from any known

[1] See Plate XIII. Fig. 1, from one of Selinus, and Fig. 3, from one of Syracuse, belonging to me.

[2] See Plate XIII. Fig. 2, from one in the collection of Mr. Townley.

[3] See Plate XIII. Fig. 3. The medal is extremely common, and the quadrangular impression is observable upon a great number of the more ancient Greek medals, generally with some symbol of the Deity in the centre. See those of Athens, Lyttus, Maronea, &c.

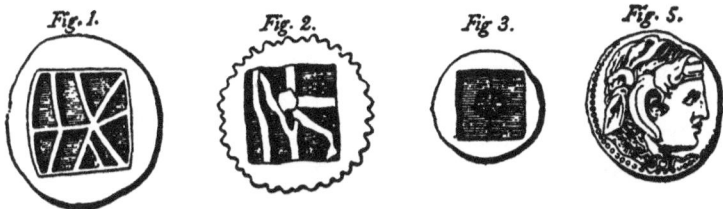

Fig. 1.

Fig. 2.

Fig 3.

Fig. 5.

Fig. 4.

Fig. 6.

Fig. 7.

Fig. 8.

Fig. 9.

Fig 10.

Fig. 11.

PLATE XIII

CELTIC TEMPLE AND GREEK MEDALS

Greek or Egyptian sculptures; but from this little Indian temple, we find that the four corners were adapted to four of the subordinate deities, or personified modes of action of the great universal Generator, represented by the symbol in the middle, to which the others are represented as paying their adorations, with gestures of humility and respect.[1]

What is the precise meaning of these four symbolical figures, it is scarcely possible for us to discover, from the small fragments of the mystic learning of the ancients which are now extant. That they were however intended as personified attributes, we can have no doubt; for we are taught by the venerable authority of the *Bagvat Geeta,* that all the subordinate deities were such, or else canonised men, which these figures evidently are not. As for the mythological tales now current in India, they throw the same degree of light upon the subject, as Ovid's Metamorphoses do on the ancient theology of Greece; that is, just enough to bewilder and perplex those who give up their attention to it. The ancient author before cited is deserving of more credit; but he has said very little upon the symbolical worship. His work, nevertheless, clearly proves that its principles were precisely the same as those of the Greeks and

[1] See Plate XII.

Egyptians, among whose remains of art or literature, we may, perhaps, find some probable analogies to aid conjecture. The elephant is, however, a new symbol in the west; the Greeks never having seen one of those animals before the expedition of Alexander,[1] although the use of ivory was familiar among them even in the days of Homer. Upon this Indian monument the head of the elephant is placed upon the body of a man with four hands, two of which are held up as prepared to strike with the instruments they hold, and the other two pointed down as in adoration of the *Lingam*. This figure is called Gonnis and Pollear by the modern Hindoos; but neither of these names is to be found in the *Geeta*, where the deity only says, *that the learned behold him alike in the reverend Brahman perfected in knowledge, in the ox, and in the elephant.* What peculiar attributes the elephant was meant to express, the ancient writer has not told us; but, as the characteristic properties of this animal are strength and sagacity, we may conclude that his image was intended to represent ideas somewhat similar to those which the Greeks represented by that of Minerva, who was worshipped as the goddess of force and wisdom, of war and counsel. The Indian Gonnis is indeed male, and Minerva fe-

[1] Pausan. lib. i. c. 12.

male; but this difference of sexes, however important it may be in a physical, is of very little consequence in metaphysical beings, Minerva being, like the other Greek deities, either male or female, or both.[1] On the medals of the Ptolemies, under whom the Indian symbols became familiar to the Greeks through the commerce of Alexandria, we find her repeatedly represented with the elephant's skin upon her head, instead of a helmet; and with a countenance between male and female, such as the artist would naturally give her, when he endeavoured to blend the Greek and Indian symbols, and mould them into one.[2] Minerva is said by the Greek mythologists to have been born without a mother from the head of Jupiter, who was delivered of her by the assistance of Vulcan. This, in plain language, means no more than that she was a pure emanation of the divine mind, operating by means of the universal agent fire, and not, like others of the allegorical personages, sprung from any of the particular operations of the deity upon external matter. Hence she is said to be next in dignity to her father, and to be endowed with all his attributes; [3] for, as wisdom is the most exalted quality of the mind, and the divine mind the perfection of

---

[1] Αρσεν και θηλνς εφνς.   Orph. εισΑθην·
[2] See Plate XIII. Fig. 5, engraved from one belonging to me.
[3] Hor. lib. 1. Od. 12. Callimach. εις Αθην·

wisdom, all its attributes are the attributes of wisdom, under whose direction its power is always exerted. Strength and wisdom therefore, when considered as attributes of the deity, are in fact one and the same. The Greek Minerva is usually represented with the spear uplifted in her hand, in the same manner as the Indian Gonnis holds the battle-axe.[1] Both are given to denote the destroying power equally belonging to divine wisdom, as the creative or preserving. The statue of Jupiter at Labranda in Caria held in his hand the battle-axe, instead of thunder; and on the medals of Tenedos and Thyatira, we find it represented alone as the symbol of the deity, in the same manner as the thunder is upon a great variety of other medals. *I am the thunderbolt*, says the deity in the *Bagvat Geeta;*[2] and when we find this supposed engine of divine vengeance upon the medals, we must not imagine that it is meant for the weapon of the supreme god, but for the symbol of his destroying attribute. What instrument the Gonnis holds in his other hand, is not easily ascertained, it being a little injured by the carriage. In one of those pointed downwards he holds the Lotus flower, to denote that he has the direction of the passive powers

[1] See Plate xiii. Fig. ii, from a medal of Seleucus I. belonging to me.
[2] Page 86.

of production; and in the other, a golden ring or disc, which, I shall soon shew, was the symbol by which many nations of the East represented the sun. His head is drawn into a conical, or pyramidal form, and surrounded by an ornament which evidently represents flames; the Indians, as well as the Greeks, looking upon fire as the essence of all active power; whence perpetual lamps are kept burning in the holy of holies of all the great pagodas in India, as they were anciently in the temple of Jupiter Ammon, and many others both Greek and Barbarian; [1] and the incarnate god in the *Bagvat Geeta* says, *I am the fire residing in the bodies of all things which have life.*[2] Upon the forehead of the Gonnis is a crescent representing the moon, whose power over the waters of the ocean caused her to be regarded as the sovereign of the great nutritive element, and whose mild rays, being accompanied by the refreshing dews and cooling breezes of the night, made her naturally appear to the inhabitants of hot countries as the comforter and restorer of the earth. *I am the moon* (says the deity in the Bagvat Geeta) *whose nature it is to give the quality of taste and relish, and to cherish the herbs and plants of the field.*[3] The light of the sun, moon,

[1] See Plut. *de Orac. defect.*
[2] Page 113.
[3] Page 113.

and fire, were however all but one, and equally emanations of the supreme being. *Know,* says the deity
in the same ancient dialogue, *that the light which
proceedeth from the sun, and illuminateth the world,
and the light which is in the moon and in the fire, are
mine. I pervade all things in nature, and guard them
with my beams.*[1] In the figure now under consideration a kind of pre-eminence seems to be given to the
moon over the sun; proceeding probably from the
Hindoos not possessing the true solar system, which
must however have been known to the people from
whom they learnt to calculate eclipses, which they
still continue to do, though upon principles not understood by themselves. They now place the earth
in the centre of the universe, as the later Greeks did,
among whom we also find the same preference given
to the lunar symbol; Jupiter being represented, on a
medal of Antiochus VIII., with the crescent upon his
head, and the asterisc of the sun in his hand.[2] In a
passage of the *Bagvat Geeta* already cited we find the
elephant and bull mentioned together as symbols of
the same kind; and on a medal of Seleucus Nicator
we find them united by the horns of the one being
placed on the head of the other.[3] The later Greeks

[1] See Plut. *de Orac. defect.*
[2] Plate xiii. Fig. 10, from one belonging to me.
[3] See Plate xiii. Fig. 9, and Gesner, *Num. Reg. Syr.* Tab. viii.
Fig. 23.

also sometimes employed the elephant as the universal symbol of the deity; in which sense he is represented on a medal of Antiochus VI. bearing the
torch, the emblem of the universal agent, fire, in his
proboscis, and the cornucopia, the result of its exertion, in his tail.[1]

On another corner of the little Indian pagoda, is a
figure with four heads, all of the same pointed form
as that of the Gonnis. This I take to represent
Brahma, to whom the Hindoos attribute four mouths,
and say that with them he dictated the four Beads,
or Veads, the mystic volumes of their religion.[2] The
four heads are turned different ways, but exactly
resemble each other. The beards have been painted
black, and are sharp and pointed, like those of goats,
which the Greeks gave to Pan, and his subordinate
emanations, the Fauns and Satyrs. Hence I am inclined to believe, that the Brahma of the Indians is
the same as the Pan of the Greeks; that is, the creative spirit of the deity transfused through matter,
and acting in the four elements represented by the
four heads. The Indians indeed admit of a fifth element, as the Greeks did likewise; but this is never
classed with the rest, being of an ætherial and more

[1] See Plate xiii. Fig. 8, and Gesner, *Num. Reg. Syr.* Tab. viii.
Fig. i.
[2] *Bagvat Geeta*, Note 41.

exalted nature, and belonging peculiarly to the deity. *Some call it heaven, some light, and some æther,* says Plutarch.[1] The Hindoos now call it *Occus,* by which they seem to mean pure ætherial light or fire.

This mode of representing the allegorical personages of religion with many heads and limbs to express their various attributes, and extensive operation, is now universal in the East,[2] and seems anciently not to have been unknown to the Greeks, at least if we may judge by the epithets used by Pindar and other early poets.[3] The union of two symbolical heads is common among the specimens of their art now extant, as may be seen upon the medals of Syracuse, Marseilles, and many other cities. Upon a gem of this sort in the collection of Mr. Townley, the same ideas which are expressed on the Indian pagoda by the distinct figures Brahma and Gonnis, are expressed by the united heads of Ammon and Minerva. Ammon, as before observed, was the Pan of the Greeks, and Minerva is here evidently the same as the Gonnis, being represented after the Indian manner, with the elephant's skin on her head, instead of a helmet.[4] Both these heads appear separate upon

[1] El apud Delph.
[2] See Kæmpfer, Chappe D'Auteroche, Sonnerat, &c.
[3] Such as ἑκατογκεφαλος, εκατοντακανος, εκατογχειρος, &c.
[4] See Plate xiii. Fig. 7.

different medals of the Ptolemies,[1] under one of whom this gem was probably engraved, Alexandria having been for a long time the great centre of religions, as well as of trade and science.

Next to the figure of Brahma on the pagoda is the cow of plenty, or the female emblem of the generative or nutritive power of the earth; and at the other corner, next to the Gonnis, is the figure of a woman, with a head of the same conic or pyramidal form, and upon the front of it a flame of fire, from which hangs a crescent.[2] This seems to be the female personification of the divine attributes represented by the Gonnis or Pollear; for the Hindoos, like the Greeks, worship the deity under both sexes, though they do not attempt to unite both in one figure. *I am the father and the mother of the world,* says the incarnate god in the *Bagvat Geeta.*[3] *Amongst cattle,* adds he in a subsequent part, *I am the cow Kamadhook. I am the prolific Kandarp, the god of love.*[4] These two sentences, by being placed together, seem to imply some relation between this *god of love* and the *cow Kamadhook;* and, were we to read the words without punctuation, as they are in all ancient or-

[1] See Plate xii. Fig. 5 and 6.
[2] See Plate xii.
[3] Page 80.
[4] Page 86.

thography, we should think the author placed the god of love amongst the cattle; which he would naturally do, if it were the custom of his religion to represent him by an animal symbol. Among the Egyptians, as before observed, the cow was the symbol of Venus, the goddess of love, and passive generative power of nature. On the capitals of one of the temples of Philæ we still find the heads of this goddess represented of a mixed form; the horns and ears of the cow being joined to the beautiful features of a woman in the prime of life; [1] such as the Greeks attributed to that Venus, whom they worshipped as the mother of the prolific god of love, Cupid, who was the personification of animal desire or concupiscence, as the Orphic love, the father of gods and men, was of universal attraction. The Greeks, who represented the mother under the form of a beautiful woman, naturally represented the son under the form of a beautiful boy; but a people who represented the mother under the form of a cow, would as naturally represent the son under the form of a calf. This seems to be the case with the Hindoos, as well as with the Egyptians; wherefore Kandarp may be very properly placed among the cattle.

By following this analogy, we may come to the

[1] See Plate xviii. Fig. 3.

PLATE XIV

PORTABLE TEMPLE DEDICATED TO PRIAPUS OR THE LINGAM

true meaning of a much-celebrated object of devotion, recorded by another ancient writer, of a more
venerable character. When the Israelites grew
clamorous on account of the absence of Moses, and
called upon Aaron to make them a god to go before
them, he set up a golden calf; to which the people
sacrificed and feasted, and then rose up (as the
translator says) *to play;* but in the original the term
is more specific, and means, in its plain direct sense,
that particular sort of play which requires the con-
currence of both sexes,[1] and which was therefore a
very proper conclusion of a sacrifice to Cupid, though
highly displeasing to the god who had brought them
out of Egypt. The Egyptian mythologists, who appeared to have invented this secondary deity of love,
were probably the inventors likewise of a secondary
Priapus, who was the personification of that particular generative faculty, which springs from animal desire, as the primary Priapus was of the great generative principle of the universe. Hence, in the allegories of the poets, this deity is said to be a son of
Bacchus and Venus; that is, the result of the active
and passive generative powers of nature. The story
of his being the son of a Grecian conqueror, and born
at Lampsacus, seems to be a corruption of this
allegory.

[1] *Exod.* xxxii.

Of all the nations of antiquity the Persians were the most simple and direct in the worship of the creator. They were the puritans of the heathen world, and not only rejected all images of god or his agents, but also temples and altars, according to Herodotus,[1] whose authority I prefer to any other, because he had an opportunity of conversing with them before they had adopted any foreign superstitions.[2] As they worshipped the ætherial fire without any medium of personification or allegory, they thought it unworthy of the dignity of the god to be represented by any definite form, or circumscribed to any particular place. The universe was his temple, and the all-pervading element of fire his only symbol. The Greeks appear originally to have held similar opinions; for they were long without statues;[3] and Pausanias speaks of a temple at Sicyon, built by Adrastus,[4] who lived an age before the Trojan war; which consisted of columns only, without wall or roof, like the Celtic temples of our Northern ancestors, or the Pyrætheia of the Persians, which were

---

[1] Lib. i.

[2] Hyde, Anquetil, and other modern writers, have given us the operose superstitions of the present Parsees for the simple theism of the ancient Persians.

[3] Pauson, lib. vii. and ix.

[4] Lib. ii.

circles of stones, in the centre of which was kindled the sacren fire,[1] the symbol of the god. Homer frequently speaks of places of worship consisting of an area and altar only (τεμενοε Βωμος τε), which were probably inclosures like these of the Persians, with an altar in the centre. The temples dedicated to the creator Bacchus, which the Greek architects called *hypaethral,* seem to have been anciently of the same kind; whence probably came the title περικιονιον (*surrounded with columns*) attributed to that god in the Orphic litanies.[2] The remains of one of these are still extant at Puzzuoli near Naples, which the inhabitants call the Temple of Serapis: but the ornaments of grapes, vases, &c. found among the ruins, prove it to have been of Bacchus. Serapis was indeed the same deity worshipped under another form, being equally a personification of the sun.[3] The architecture is of the Roman times; but the ground plan is probably that of a very ancient one, which this was made to replace; for it exactly resembles that of a Celtic temple in Zeeland, published in Stukeley's *itinerary.*[4] The ranges of square buildings which inclose it are not properly parts of the

[1] Strab. lib. xv.
[2] Hymn. 46.
[3] Diodor. Sic. lib. i. Macrob. *Sat.* lib. i. c. 20.
[4] See Plate xv. Fig. 1 and 2, and Plate xiii. Fig. 4.

temple, but apartments of the priests, places for victims and sacred utensils, and chapels dedicated to subordinate deities introduced by a more complicated and corrupt worship, and probably unknown to the founders of the original edifice.[1] The portico, which runs parallel with these buildings,[2] inclosed the *temenos,* or area of sacred ground, which in the *pyræthia* of the Persians was circular, but is here quadrangular, as in the Celtic temple in Zeeland, and the Indian pagoda before described. In the centre was the holy of holies, the seat of the god, consisting of a circle of columns raised upon a basement, without roof or walls, in the middle of which was probably the sacred fire, or some other symbol of the deity.[3] The square area in which it stood, was sunk below the natural level of the ground,[4] and, like that of the little Indian pagoda, appears to have been occasionally floated with water, the drains and conduits being still to be seen,[5] as also several fragments of sculpture representing waves, serpents, and various aquatic animals, which once adorned the basement.[6] The Bacchus περικιονιος here worshipped, was,

[1] Plate xv. Fig. 2, *a—a.*
[2] Plate xv. Fig. 2, *b—b.*
[3] See Plate xv. Fig. I, *a,* and Fig. 2, *c.*
[4] See Plate xv. Fig. I, *b—b.*
[5] See Plate xv. Fig. I, *c—c.*
[6] See Plate xvii. Fig. I.

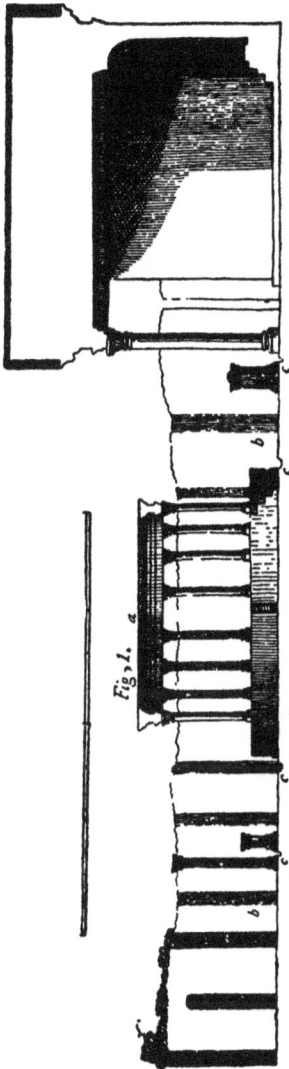

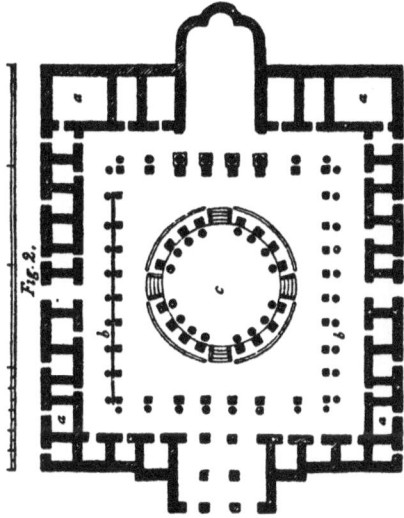

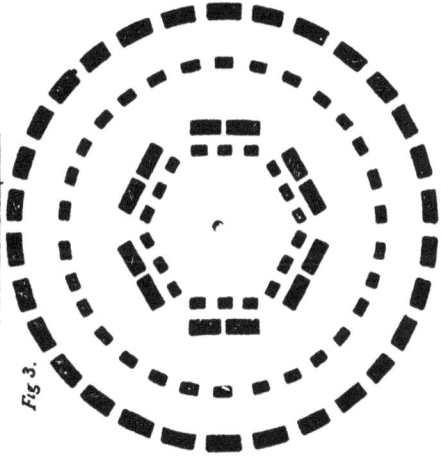

Fig. 2.

Fig. 1.

Fig. 3.

PLATE XV

TEMPLE DEDICATED TO BACCHUS AT PUZZUOLI

as we learn from the Orphic hymn above cited, the sun in his character of extinguisher of the fires which once pervaded the earth. This he was supposed to have done by exhaling the waters of the ocean, and scattering them over the land, which was thus supposed to have acquired its proper temperature and fertility. For this reason the sacred fire, the essential image of the god, was surrounded by the element which was principally employed in giving effect to the beneficial exertions of his great attribute.

These Orphic temples were, without doubt, emblems of that fundamental principle of the mystic faith of the ancients, the solar system; fire, the essence of the deity, occupying the place of the sun, and the columns surrounding it as the subordinate parts of the universe. Remains of the worship of fire continued among the Greeks even to the last, as appears from the sacred fires kept in the interior apartment, or holy of holies, of almost all their temples, and places of worship: and, though the Ammonian Platonics, the last professors of the ancient religion, endeavoured to conceive something beyond the reach of sense and perception, as the essence of their supreme god; yet, when they wanted to illustrate and explain the modes of action of this metaphysical abstraction, who was more subtle than intelligence itself, they do it by images and comparisons of light and fire.[1]

From a passage of Hecatæus, preserved by Diodorus Siculus, I think it is evident that Stonehenge, and all the other monuments of the same kind found in the North, belonged to the same religion, which appears, at some remote period, to have prevailed over the whole northern hemisphere. According to that ancient historian, *the Hyperboreans inhabited an island beyond Gaul, as large as Sicily, in which Apollo was worshipped in a circular temple considerable for its size and riches.*[2] Apollo, we know, in the language of the Greeks of that age, can mean no other than the sun, which, according to Cæsar, was worshipped by the Germans, when they knew of no other deities except fire and the moon.[3] The island I think can be no other than Britain, which at that time was only known to the Greeks by the vague reports of Phœnician mariners, so uncertain and obscure, that Herodotus, the most inquisitive and credulous of historians, doubts of its existence.[4] The circular temple of the sun being noticed in such

[1] See Proclus. *in Theol. Platon.* lib. i. c. 19.

[2] Ναον αξιολογον, αναθημασι πολλοις κεκοσ μημενον, σφαιροειδη τωσχηματι. Diod. Sic. lib. ii.

[3] *De B. Gal.* lib. vi.

[4] Lib. iii. c. 15.

Fig. 1.

Fig. 2.

PLATE XVI
ORNAMENT FROM PUZZUOLI TEMPLE

slight and imperfect accounts, proves that it must have been something singular and important; for, if it had been an inconsiderable structure, it would not have been mentioned at all; and, if there had been many such in the country, the historian would not have employed the singular number. Stonehenge has certainly been a circular temple, nearly the same as that already described of the Bacchus περικιονιος at Puzzuoli, except that in the latter the nice execution, and beautiful symmetry of the parts, are in every respect the reverse of the rude but majestic simplicity of the former; in the original design they differ but in the form of the area.[1] It may therefore be reasonably supposed, that we have still the ruins of the identical temple described by Hecatæus, who, being an Asiatic Greek, might have received his information from some Phœnician merchant, who had visited the interior parts of Britain when trading there for tin. Macrobius mentions a temple of the same kind and form upon Mount Zilmissus in Thrace,

[1] See Plate xv. Fig. 2 and 3. I have preferred Webb's plan of Stonehenge to Stukeley's and Smith's, after comparing each with the ruins now existing. They differ materially only in the cell, which Webb supposes to have been a hexagon, and Stukeley a section of an ellipsis. The position of the altar is merely conjectural; wherefore I have omitted it; and I much doubt whether either be right in their plans of the cell, which seems, as in other Druidical temples, to have been meant for a circle, but incorrectly executed.

dedicated to the sun under the title of Bacchus Sebazius.[1] The large obeliscs of stone found in many parts of the North, such as those at Rudstone,[2] and near Boroughbridge in Yorkshire,[3] belong to the same religion; obeliscs being, as Pliny observes, sacred to the sun, whose rays they represented both by their form and name.[4] An ancient medal of Apollonia in Illyria, belonging to the Museum of the late Dr. Hunter, has the head of Apollo crowned with laurel on one side, and on the other an obelisc terminating in a cross, the least explicit representation of the male organs of generation.[5] This has exactly the appearance of one of those crosses, which were erected in church-yards and cross roads for the adoration of devout persons, when devotion was more prevalent than at present. Many of these were undoubtedly erected before the establishment of Christianity, and converted, together with their worshippers, to the true faith. Anciently they represented the generative power of light, the essence of God; *for God is light, and never but in unapproached light dwelt from*

[1] *Sat.* lib. i. c. 18.

[2] *Archaeologia*, vol. v.

[3] Now called the Devil's Arrows. See Stukeley's *Itin.* vol. i. Table xc.

[4] *Hist. Nat.* lib. xxxvi. sec. 14.

[5] Plate x. Fig. 1, and *Nummi Pop. & Urb.* Table x. Fig. 7.

eternity, says Milton, who in this, as well as many other instances, has followed the Ammonian Platonics, who were both the restorers and corrupters of the ancient theology. They restored it from the mass of poetical mythology, under which it was buried, but refined and sublimated it with abstract metaphysics, which soared as far above human reason as the poetical mythology sunk below it. From the ancient solar obeliscs came the spires and pinnacles with which our churches are still decorated, so many ages after their mystic meaning has been forgotten. Happily for the beauty of these edifices, it was forgotten; otherwise the reformers of the last century would have destroyed them, as they did the crosses and images; for they might with equal propriety have been pronounced heathenish and prophane.

As the obelisc was the symbol of light, so was the pyramid of fire, deemed to be essentially the same. The Egyptians, among whom these forms are the most frequent, held that there were two opposite powers in the world, perpetually acting contrary to each other, the one creating, and the other destroying: the former they called Osiris, and the latter Typhon.[1] By the contention of these two, that mix-

[1] Plutarch. *de Is. & Os.*

ture of good and evil, which, according to some verses of Euripides quoted by Plutarch,[1] constituted the harmony of the world, was supposed to be produced. This opinion of the necessary mixture of good and evil was, according to Plutarch, of immemorial antiquity, derived from the oldest theologists and legislators, not only in traditions and reports, but in mysteries and sacrifices, both Greek and barbarian.[2] Fire was the efficient principle of both, and, according to some of the Egyptians, that ætherial fire which concentred in the sun. This opinion Plutarch controverts, saying that Typhon, the evil or destroying power, was a terrestrial or material fire, essentially different from the ætherial. But Plutarch here argues from his own prejudices, rather than from the evidence of the case; for he believed in an original evil principle coeternal with the good, and acting in perpetual opposition to it; an error into which men have been led by forming false notions of good and evil, and considering them as self-existing inherent properties, instead of accidental modifications, variable with every circumstance with which causes and events are connected. This error, though adopted by individuals, never formed a part either of the the-

[1] Plutarch. de Is. & Os.
[2] Ibid. Ed. Reiskii.

ology or mythology of Greece. Homer, in the beautiful allegory of the two casks, makes Jupiter, the supreme god, the distributor of both good and evil.[1] The name of Jupiter, Ζευς, was originally one of the titles or epithets of the sun, signifying, according to its etymology, *aweful* or *terrible;*[2] in which sense it is used in the Orphic litanies.[3] Pan, the universal substance, is called the horned Jupiter (Ζευς ο κεραστης); and in an Orphic fragment preserved by Macrobius[4] the names of Jupiter and Bacchus appear to be only titles of the all-creating power of the sun.

> Αγλαε Ζεν, Διοννσε, πατεζ ποντον, πατεζ αιης,
> 'Ηλιε παγγενετοζ.

In another fragment preserved by the same author,[5] the name of Pluto, Αιδης, is used as a title of the same deity; who appears therefore to have presided over the dead as well as over the living, and to have been the lord of destruction as well as creation and preservation. We accordingly find that in one of the Orphic litanies now extant, he is expressly called the giver of life, and the destroyer.[6]

[1] *Il. w,* v. 527.
[2] Damm. *Lex. Etymol.*
[3] Hymn. x. v. 13.
[4] *Sat.* lib. 1. c. 23.
[5] *Sat.* lib. 1. c. 8 .
[6] Hymn. lxxii. *Ed. Gesn.*

The Egyptians represented Typhon, the destroying power, under the figure of the hippopotamus or river-horse, the most fierce and destructive animal they knew; [1] and the Chorus in the *Bacchae* of Euripides invoke their inspirer Bacchus to appear under the form of a bull, a many-headed serpent, or flaming lion; [2] which shews that the most bloody and destructive, as well as the most useful of animals, was employed by the Greeks to represent some personified attribute of the god. M. D'Hancarville has also observed, that the lion is frequently employed by the ancient artists as a symbol of the sun; [3] and I am inclined to believe that it was to express this destroying power, no less requisite to preserve the harmony of the universe than the generating. In most of the monuments of ancient art where the lion is represented, he appears with expressions of rage and violence, and often in the act of killing and devouring some other animal. On an ancient sarcophagus found in Sicily he is represented devouring a horse, [4] and on the medals of Velia in Italy, devouring a deer; [5] the former, as sacred to Neptune, represented

[1] Plutarch. *de Is. & Os.*
[2] V. 1015.
[3] *Recherches sur les Arts.* See also Macrob. *Sat.* i. c. 21.
[4] Houel, *Voyage de la Sicile.* Plate xxxvi.
[5] Plate ix. Fig. 5, engraved from one belonging to me.

PLATE XVII
ORNAMENT FROM PUZZUOLI TEMPLE

the sea; and the latter, as sacred to Diana, the produce of the earth; for Diana was the fertility of the earth personified, and therefore is said to have received her nymphs or productive ministers from the ocean, the source of fecundity.[1] The lion, therefore, in the former instance, appears as a symbol of the sun exhaling the waters; and in the latter, as withering and putrifying the produce of the earth. On the frieze of the Temple of Apollo Didymæus, near Miletus, are monsters composed of the mixt forms of the goat and lion, resting their fore feet upon the lyre of the god, which stands between them.[2] The goat, as I have already shewn, represented the creative attribute, and the lyre, harmony and order; therefore, if we admit that the lion represented the destroying attribute, this composition will signify, in the symbolical language of sculpture, the harmony and order of the universe preserved by the regular and periodical operations of the creative and destructive powers. This is a notion to which men would be naturally led by observing the common order and progression of things. The same heat of the sun, which scorched and withered the grass in summer, ripened the fruits in autumn, and cloathed the earth

[1] Callimach. *Hymn ad Dian.* v. 13. *Genitor Nympharum Oceanus.* Catullus *in Gell.* v. 84.
[2] *Ionian Antiquities,* vol. i. c. 3. Plate IX.

with verdure in the spring. In one season it dried up the waters from the earth, and in another returned them in rain. It caused fermentation and putrefaction, which destroy one generation of plants and animals, and produce another in constant and regular succession. This contention between the powers of creation and destruction is represented on an ancient medal of Acanthus, in the museum of the late Dr. Hunter, by a combat between the bull and lion.[1] The bull alone is represented on other medals in exactly the same attitude and gesture as when fighting with the lion;[2] whence I conclude that the lion is there understood. On the medals of Celenderis, the goat appears instead of the bull in exactly the same attitude of struggle and contention, but without the lion;[3] and in a curious one of very ancient but excellent workmanship, belonging to me, the ivy of Bacchus is placed over the back of the goat, to denote the power which he represents.[4]

The mutual operation which was the result of this contention was signified, in the mythological tales of the poets, by the loves of Mars and Venus, the one

[1] Plate IX. Fig. 4, & *Nummi Vet. Pop. & Urb.* Table I. Fig. 16.

[2] Plate IX. Fig. 12, from one of Aspendus in the same Collection. See *Nummi Vet. Pop. & Urb.* Table VIII. Fig. 20.

[3] *Nummi Vet. Pop. & Urb.* Table XVI. Fig. 13.

[4] Plate IX. Fig. 13.

the active power of destruction, and the other the passive power of generation. From their union is said to have sprung the goddess *Harmony*, who was the physical order of the universe personified. The fable of Ceres and Proserpine is the same allegory inverted; Ceres being the prolific power of the earth personified, and hence called by the Greeks *Mother Earth* (Γη or Λη-μητης). The Latin name Ceres also signifying *Earth*, the Roman C being the same originally, both in figure and power as the Greek Γ,[1] which Homer often uses as a mere guttural aspirate, and adds it arbitrarily to his words, to make them more solemn and sonorous.[2] The guttural aspirates and hissing terminations more particularly belonged to the Æolic dialect, from which the Latin was derived; wherefore we need not wonder that the same word, which by the Dorians and Ionians was written Εϱα and Εϱε, should by the Æolians be written Γεϱες or Ceres, the Greeks always accommodating their orthography to their pronunciation. In an ancient bronze at Strawberry Hill this goddess is represented sitting, with a cup in one hand, and various sorts of fruits in the other; and the bull, the emblem of the power of the Creator, in her lap.[3] This composition

---

[1] See S. C. Marcian, and the medals of Gela and Agrigentum.
[2] As in the word εϱιδϕπος, usually written by him εϱιγδϕπος.
[3] See Plate viii.

shews the fructification of the earth by the descent of
the creative spirit in the same manner as described
by Virgil:—

> Vere tument terræ, et genitalia semina posuunt;
> Tum pater omnipotens fœcundis imbribus æther
> Conjugis in gremium lætæ descendit, & omnes
> Magnus alit, magno commixtus corpore, fœtus.[1]

Æther and water are here introduced by the poet as
the two prolific elements which fertilize the earth,
according to the ancient system of Orphic philosophy, upon which the mystic theology was
founded. Proserpine, or Περσιφονεια, the daughter of
Ceres, was, as her Greek name indicates, the goddess
of destruction, in which character she is invoked by
Althæa in the ninth Iliad; but nevertheless we often
find her on the Greek medals crowned with ears of
corn, as being the goddess of fertility as well as
destruction.[2] She is, in fact, a personification of the
heat or fire that pervades the earth, which is at once
the cause and effect of fertility and destruction, for
it is at once the cause and effect of fermentation,
from which both proceed. The Libitina, or goddess
of death of the Romans, was the same as the Persiphoneia of the Greeks; and yet, as Plutarch observes,

[1] *Georgic.* lib. ii. .v. 324.
[2] Plate iv. Fig. 5, from a medal of Agathocles, belonging to me.
The same head is upon many others, of Syracuse, Metapontum, &c.

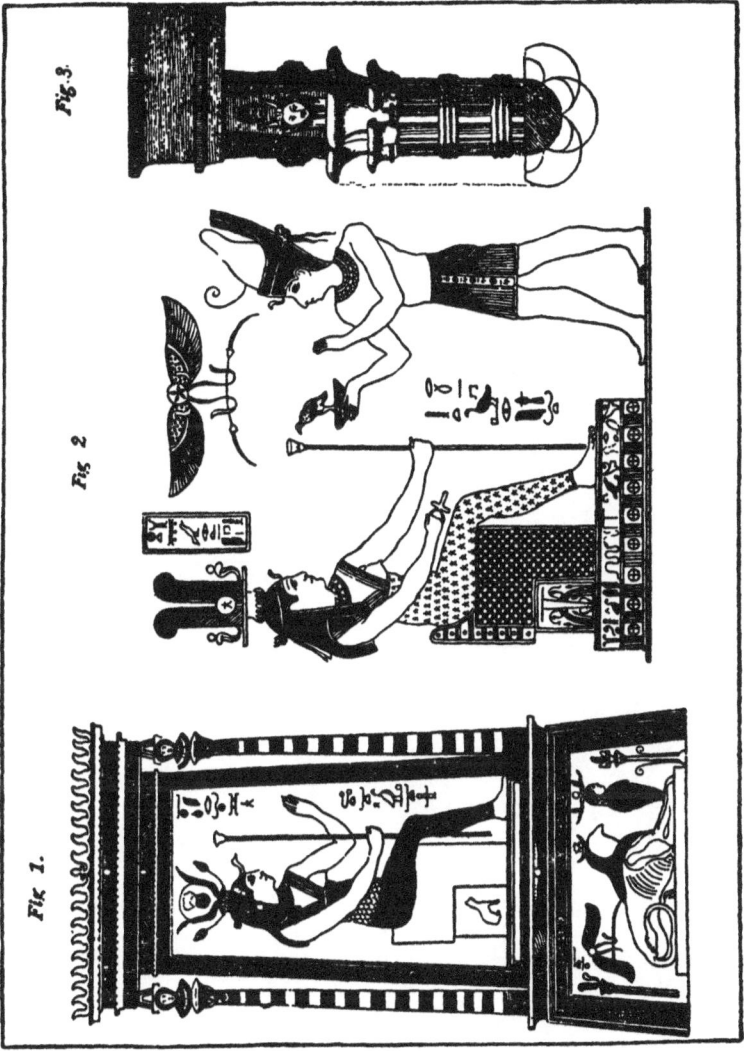

PLATE XVIII

EGYPTIAN FIGURES AND ORNAMENTS

the most learned of that people allowed her to be the same as Venus, the goddess of generation.[1]

In the Gallery at Florence is a collossal image of the organ of generation, mounted on the back parts of a lion, and hung round with various animals. By this is represented the co-operation of the creating and destroying powers, which are both blended and united in one figure, because both are derived from one cause. The animals hung round show likewise that both act to the same purpose, that of replenishing the earth, and peopling it with still rising generations of sensitive beings. The Chimæra of Homer, of which the commentators have given so many whimsical interpretations, was a symbol of the same kind, which the poet probably, having seen in Asia, and not knowing its meaning (which was only revealed to the initiated) supposed to be a monster that had once infested the country. He describes it as composed of the forms of the *goat*, the *lion*, and the *serpent*, and breathing *fire* from its mouth.[2] These are the symbols of the *creator*, the *destroyer*, and the *preserver*, united and animated by *fire*, the divine essence of all *three*.[3] On a gem, published in the

[1] In Numa.

[2] *Il.* ζ. v. 223.

[3] For the natural properties attributed by the ancients to fire, see Plutarch, *in Camillo*, Plin. *Hist. Nat.* lib. xxxvi. c. 68.

Memoirs of the Academy of Cortona,[1] this union of the destroying and preserving attributes is represented by the united forms of the lion and serpent crowned with rays, the emblems of the cause from which both proceed. This composition forms the Chnoubis of the Egyptians.

Bacchus is frequently represented by the ancient artists accompanied by tigers, which appear, in some instances, devouring clusters of grapes, the fruit peculiarly consecrated to the god, and in others drinking the liquor pressed from them. The author of the *Recherches sur les Arts* has in this instance followed the common accounts of the Mythologists, and asserted that tigers are really fond of grapes; [2] which is so far from being true, that they are incapable of feeding upon them, or upon any fruit whatever, being both externally and internally formed to feed upon flesh only, and to procure their food by destroying other animals. Hence I am persuaded, that in the ancient symbols, tigers, as well as lions, represent the destroying power of the god. Sometimes his chariot appears drawn by them; and then they represent the powers of destruction preceding the powers of generation, and extending their operation, as putrefaction precedes, and increases vegetation. On

[1] Vol. iv. p. 32. See also Plate v. Fig. 4, copied from it.
[2] Liv. 1. c. 3.

a medal of Maronea, published by Gesner,[1] a goat is coupled with the tiger in drawing his chariot; by which composition the artist has shewn the *general active* power of the deity, conducted by his two great attributes of creation and destruction. On the Choragic monument of Lysicrates at Athens, Bacchus is represented feeding a tiger; which shows the active power of destruction.[2] On a beautiful cameo in the collection of the Duke of Marlborough, the tiger is sucking the breast of a nymph; which represents the same power of destruction, nourished by the passive power of generation.[3] In the museum of Charles Townley, Esq., is a group, in marble, of three figures;[4] the middle one of which grows out of a vine in a human form, with leaves and clusters of grapes springing out of its body. On one side is the Bacchus διφνης, or creator of both sexes, known by the effeminate mold of his limbs and countenance; and on the other, a tiger, leaping up, and devouring the grapes which spring from the body of the personified vine, the hands of which are employed in receiving

[1] Table xliii. Fig. 26.

[2] Stuart's *Athens*, vol. i. c. 4, Plate x.

[3] See Plate xxiii. engraved merely to show the composition, it not being permitted to make an exact drawing of it.

[4] See Plate xxi. Fig. 7.

another cluster from the Bacchus. This composition represents the vine between the creating and destroying attributes of god; the one giving it fruit, and the other devouring it when given. The tiger has a garland of ivy round his neck, to show that the destroyer was co-essential with the creator, of whom ivy, as well as all other ever-greens, was an emblem representing his perpetual youth and viridity.[1]

The mutual and alternate operation of the two great attributes of creation and destruction, was not confined by the ancients to plants and animals, and such transitory productions, but extended to the universe itself. Fire being the essential cause of both, they believed that the conflagration and renovation of the world were periodical and regular, proceeding from each other by the laws of its own constitution, implanted in it by the creator, who was also the destroyer and renovator;[2] for, as Plato says, all things arise from one, and into one are all things resolved.[3] It must be observed, that, when the ancients speak of creation and destruction, they mean only formation

[1] Strabo, lib. xv. p. 712.

[2] Brucker, *Hist. Crit. Philos.* vol. i. part 2, lib. i. Plutarch *de Placit. Philos.* lib. ii. c. 18. Lucretius, lib. v. ver. 92. Cic. *de Nat. Deor.* lib. ii.

[3] Εξ ενος τα παντα γενεσθαι, και εις τ' αυτον αναλυεσθαι, in Phæd. The same dogma is still more plainly inculcated by the ancient Indian author before cited, see *Bagvat Geeta*, Lect. ix.

and dissolution; it being universally allowed, through all systems of religion, or sects of philosophy, that *nothing could come from nothing, and that no power whatever could annihilate that which really existed.* The bold and magnificent idea of a creation from nothing was reserved for the more vigorous faith, and more enlightened minds of the moderns,[1] who need seek no authority to confirm their belief; for, as that which is self-evident admits of no proof, so that which is in itself impossible admits of no refutation.

The fable of the serpent Pytho being destroyed by Apollo, probably arose from an emblematical composition, in which that god was represented as the destroyer of life, of which the serpent was a symbol. Pliny mentions a statue of him by Praxiteles, which was much celebrated in his time, called Σαυροκτων (*the Lizard-killer.*)[2] The lizard, being supposed to live upon the dews and moisture of the earth, is employed as the symbol of humidity in general; so that the god destroying it, signifies the same as the lion devouring the horse. The title Apollo, I

[1] The word in *Genesis* upon which it is founded, conveyed no such sense to the ancients; for the Seventy translated it εποιησε, which signifies *formed,* or *fashioned.*

[2] *Hist. Nat.* lib. xxxiv. c. 8. Many copies of it are still extant. Winkleman has published one from a bronze of Cardinal Albani's. *Monum. Antichi. inediti,* Plate xl.

am inclined to believe, meant originally the Destroyer, as well as the Deliverer; for, as the ancients supposed destruction to be merely dissolution, the power which delivered the particles of matter from the bonds of attraction, and broke the δεσμον περιβριθη ερωτος, was in fact the destroyer.[1] It is, probably, for this reason, that sudden death, plagues, and epidemic diseases, are said by the poets to be sent by this god; who is, at the same time, described as the author of medicine, and all the arts employed to preserve life. These attributes are not joined merely because the destroyer and preserver were essentially the same; but because disease necessarily precedes cure, and is the cause of its being invented. The God of Health is said to be his son, because the health and vigour of one being are supported by the decay and dissolution of others which are appropriated to its nourishment. The bow and arrows are given to him as symbols of his characteristic attributes, as they are to Diana, who was the female personification of the destructive, as well as the productive and preserving powers. Diana is hence called the triple Hecate, and represented by three female bodies

---

[1] The verb λυω, from which Apollo is derived, signifies in Homer both to *free* and to dissolve or destroy, *Il. a, ver.* 20; *Π, ι,* ver. 25. Macrobius derives the title from απολλυμι, to *destroy;* but this word is derived from λυω Sat. lib. i. c. 17.

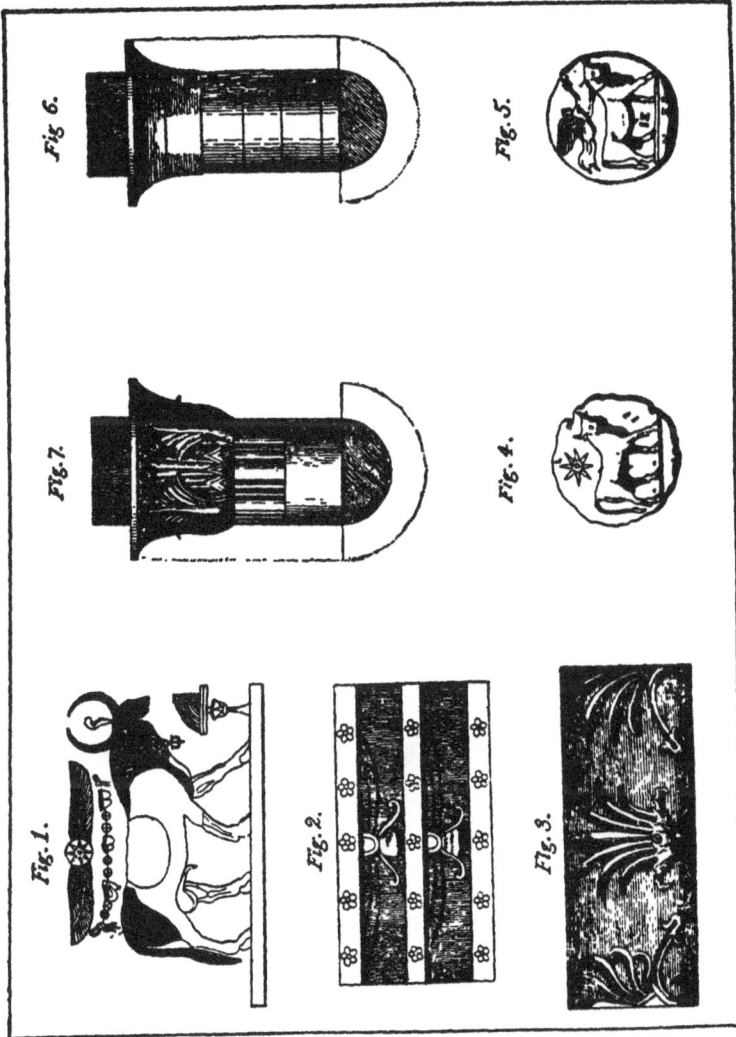

PLATE XIX

EGYPTIAN FIGURES AND ORNAMENTS

joined together. Her attributes were however worshippd separately; and some nations revered her under one character, and others under another. Diana of Ephesus was the productive and nutritive power, as the many breasts and other symbols on her statues imply; [1] whilst Βριμω, the *Tauric* or *Scythic* Diana, apears to have been the destructive, and therefore was appeased with human sacrifices, and other bloody rites.[2] She is represented sometimes standing on the back of a bull,[3] and sometimes in a chariot drawn by bulls; [4] whence she is called by the poets Ταυροπολα [5] and Βοων ελατειρα.[6]. Both compositions show the passive power of nature, whether creative or destructive, sustained and guided by the general active power of the creator, of which the sun was the centre, and the bull the symbol.

It was observed by the ancients, that the destructive power of the sun was exerted most by day, and the creative by night: for it was in the former season that he dried up the waters, withered the herbs, and

---

[1] Hieron. *Comment. in* Paul *Epist. ad Ephes.*

[2] Pausan. lib. iii. c. 16.

[3] See a medal of Augustus, published by Spanheim. *Not. in* Callim. *Hymn. ad Dian.* ver. 113.

[4] Plate vi., from a bronze in the museum of C. Townley, Esq.

[5] Sophoclis *Ajax*, ver. 172.

[6] *Nonni* Dionys, lib. i. the title Ταυροπολος was sometimes given to Apollo, Eustath. *Schol in* Dionys. Περιηγησ., ver. 609.

produced disease and putrefaction; and in the latter, that he returned the exhalations in dews, tempered with the genial heat which he had transfused into the atmosphere, to restore and replenish the waste of the day. Hence, when they personified the attributes, they revered the one as the *diurnal,* and the other as the *nocturnal* sun, and in their mystic worship, as Macrobius says,[1] called the former Apollo, and the latter Dionysus or Bacchus. The mythological personages of Castor and Pollux, who lived and died alternately, were allegories of the same dogma; hence the two asteriscs, by which they are distinguished on the medals of Locri, Argos, and other cities.

The pæans, or war-songs, which the Greeks chanted at the onset of their battles,[2] were originally sung to Apollo,[3] who was called Pæon; and Macrobius tells us,[4] that in Spain, the sun was worshipped as Mars, the god of war and destruction, whose statue they adorned with rays, like that of the Greek Apollo. On a Celtiberian or Runic medal found in Spain, of barbarous workmanship, is a head surrounded by

[1] Sat. lib. l. c. 18.
[2] Thucyd. lib. vii.
[3] Homer. *Il. a,* v. 472.
[4] Sat. lib. l. c. 19.

obeliscs or rays, which I take to be of this deity.[1] The hairs appear erect, to imitate flames, as they do on many of the Greek medals; and on the reverse is a bearded head, with a sort of pyramidal cap on, exactly resembling that by which the Romans conferred freedom on their slaves, and which was therefore called the cap of liberty.[2] On other Celtiberian medals is a figure on horseback, carrying a spear in his hand, and having the same sort of cap on his head, with the word Helman written under him,[3] in characters which are something between the old Runic and Pelasgian; but so near to the latter, that they are easily understood.[4] This figure seems to be of the same person as is represented by the head with the cap on the preceding medal, who can be no other than the angel or minister of the deity of death, as the name implies; for Hela or Hel, was, among the

[1] Plate x Fig. 2, engraven from one belonging to me. I have since been confirmed in this conjecture by observing the characters of Mars and Apollo mixt on Greek coins. On a Mamertine one belonging to me is the head with the youthful features and laurel crown of Apollo; but the hair is short, and the inscription on the exergue denotes it to be Mars. See Plate xvi. Fig 2.

[2] It may be seen with the dagger on the medals of Brutus.

[3] See Plate ix. Fig. 9, from one belonging to me.

[4] The first is a mixture of the Runic *Hagle* and Greek H. The second is the Runic *Laugur*, which is also the old Greek Λ, as it appears on the vase of the Calydonian Boar in the British Museum. The other three differ little from the common Greek.

Northern nations, the goddess of death,[1] in the same manner as Persiphoneia or Brimo was among the Greeks. The same figure appears on many ancient British medals, and also on those of several Greek cities, particularly those of Gela, which have the Taurine Bacchus or Creator on the reverse.[2] The head which I have supposed to be the Celtiberian Mars, or destructive power of the diurnal sun, is beardless like the Apollo of the Greeks, and, as far as can be discovered in such barbarous sculpture, has the same androgynous features.[3] We may therefore reasonably suppose, that, like the Greeks, the Celtiberians personified the destructive attribute under the different genders, accordingly as they applied it to the sun, or subordinate elements; and then united them, to signify that both were essentially the same. The Helman therefore, who was the same as the Μοιραγητης or Διακτωζ of the Greeks, may with equal propriety be called the minister of *both* or *either*. The spear in his hand is not to be considered merely as the implement of destruction, but as the symbol of power and command, which it was in Greece and Italy, as well as all over the North. Hence ευθυνειν

[1] Edda. Fab. XVI. *D'Hancarville, Recherches sur les Arts,* liv. ii. c. I.

[2] See Plate IX. Fig. II, from one belonging to me.

[3] See Plate X. Fig. 2.

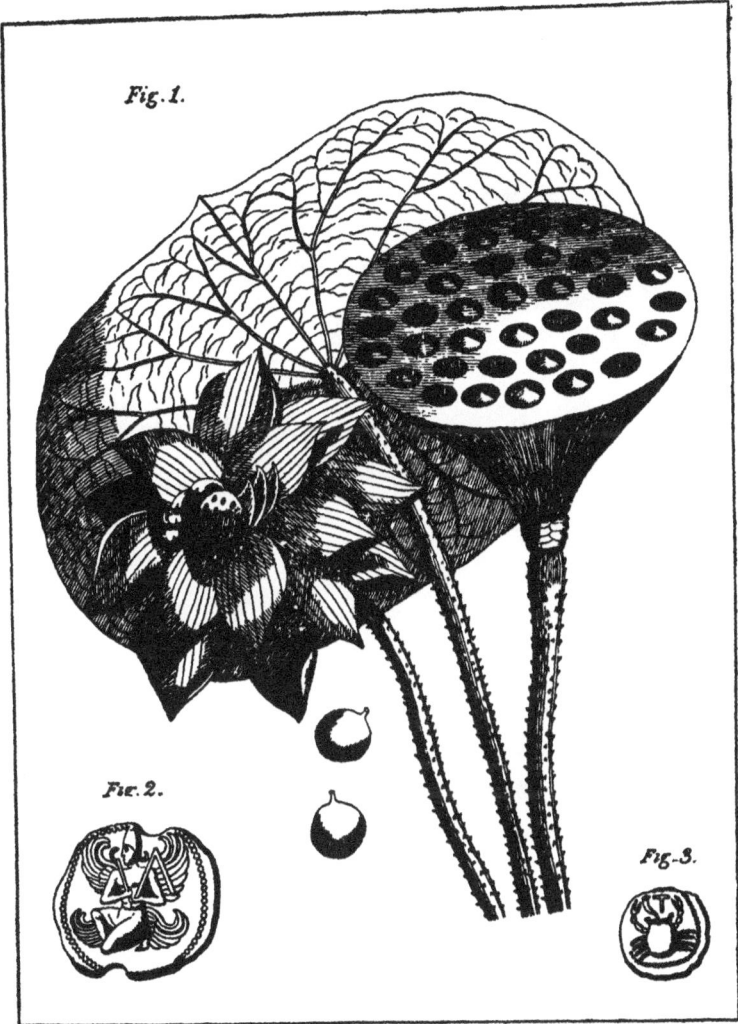

Fig. 1.

Fig. 2.

Fig. 3.

PLATE XX

THE LOTUS AND MEDALS OF MELITA

δοϱι *was to govern,*[1] and *venire sub hastâ,—to be sold as a slave.* The ancient Celtes and Scythians paid divine honors to the sword, the battle-axe, and the spear; the first of which was the symbol by which they represented the supreme god: hence to swear by the edge of the sword was the most sacred and inviolable of oaths.[2] Euripides alludes to this ancient religion when he calls a sword οϱχιον ξιφος; and Æschylus shows clearly, that it once prevailed in Greece, when he makes the heroes of the Thebaid swear by the point of the spear (ομνυσι δ'αιχμην[3]). Homer sometimes uses the word αϱης to signify the God of War, and sometimes a weapon: and we have sufficient proof of this word's being of Celtic origin in its affinity with our Northern word *War;* for, if we write it in the ancient manner, with the Pelasgian *Vau,* or Æolian *Digamma,* Fαϱης (*Wares*), it scarcely differs at all.

Behind the bearded head, on the first-mentioned Celtiberian medal is an instrument like a pair of fire-tongs, or blacksmith's pincers;[4] from which it seems that the personage here represented is the same as the 'Ηφαιστος or Vulcan of the Greek and Roman

1 Eurip. *Hecuba.*
2 Mallet, *Introd. à l'Hist. de Danemarc,* c. 9.
3 'Επταοπι Θη Βαϲ, v. 535.
4 Plate x. Fig. 2.

mythology. The same ideas are expressed somewhat more plainly on the medals of Æsernia in Italy, which are executed with all the refinement and elegance of Grecian art.[1] On one side is Apollo, the diurnal sun, mounting in his chariot; and on the other a beardless head, with the same cap on, and the same instrument behind it, but with the youthful features and elegant character of countenance usually attributed to Mercury, who, as well as Vulcan, was the God of Art and Mechanism; and whose peculiar office it also was to conduct the souls of the deceased to their eternal mansions, from whence came the epithet Διαχτωζ, applied to him by Homer. He was, therefore, in this respect, the same as the Helman of the Celtes and Scythians, who was supposed to conduct the souls of all who died a violent death (which alone was accounted truly happy) to the palace of Valhala.[2] It seems that the attributes of the deity which the Greeks represented by the mythological personages of Vulcan and Mercury, were united in the Celtic mythology. Cæsar tells us that the Germans worshipped Vulcan, or fire, with the sun and moon; and I shall soon have occasion to show that the Greeks held fire to be the real con-

[1] See Plate x. Fig. 6, from one belonging to me.
[2] Mallet, *Hist. de Danemarc. Introd. c. 9.*

ductor of the dead, and emancipator of the soul. The Æsernians, bordering upon the Samnites, a Celtic nation, might naturally be supposed to have adopted the notions of their neighbours, or, what is more probable, preserved the religion of their ancestors more pure than the Hellenic Greeks. Hence they represented Vulcan, who, from the inscription on the exergue of their coins, appears to have been their tutelar god, with the characteristic features of Mercury, who was only a different personification of the same deity.

At Lycopolis in Egypt the destroying power of the sun was represented by a wolf; which, as Macrobius says, was worshipped there as Apollo.[1] The wolf appears devouring grapes in the ornaments of the temple of Bacchus περικιονιος at Puzzuoli;[2] and on the medals of Cartha he is surrounded with rays, which plainly proves that he is there meant as a symbol of the sun.[3] He is also represented on most of the coins of Argos,[4] where I have already shown that the diurnal sun Apollo, the light-extending god, was peculiarly worshipped. We may therefore conclude, that this animal is meant for one of the mys-

[1] *Sat.* lib. i. c. 17.
[2] Plate xvi. Fig. i.
[3] Plate x, Fig. 8, from one belonging to me.
[4] Plate ix, Fig. 7, from one belonging to me.

tic symbols of the primitive worship, and not, as some antiquarians have supposed, to commemorate the mythological tales of Danaus or Lycaon, which were probably invented, like many others of the same kind, to satisfy the inquisitive ignorance of the vulgar, from whom the meaning of the mystic symbols, the usual devices on the medals, was strictly concealed. In the Celtic mythology, the same symbol was employed, apparently in the same sense, Lok, the great destroying power of the universe, being represented under the form of a wolf.[1]

The Apollo Didymæus, or *double Apollo*, was probably the two personifications, that of the *destroying*, and that of the creating power, united; whence we may perceive the reason why the ornaments before described should be upon his temple.[2] On the medals of Antigonus, king of Asia, is a figure with his hair hanging in artificial ringlets over his shoulders, like that of a woman, and the whole composition, both of his limbs and countenance, remarkable for extreme delicacy, and feminine elegance.[3] He is sitting on the prow of a ship, as god of the waters; and we should, without hesitation, pronounce him to be

[1] Mallet, *Introd. à l'Hist. de Danemarc.*
[2] See *Ionian Antiq.* vol. 1. c. 3, Pl. IX.
[3] See Plate X. Fig. 7, from one belonging to me. Similar figures are on the coins of most of the Seleucidæ.

the Bacchus διφυης, were it not for the bow that he carries in his hand, which evidently shows him to be Apollo. This I take to be the figure under which the refinement of art (and more was never shown than in this medal) represented the Apollo Didymæus, or union of the creative and destructive powers of both sexes in one body.

As fire was the primary essence of the active or male powers of creation and generation, so was water of the passive or female. Appian says, that the goddess worshipped at Hierapolis in Syria was *called by some* Venus, *by others* Juno, *and by others held to be the cause which produced the beginning and seeds of things from humidity.*[1] Plutarch describes her nearly in the same words;[2] and the author of the treatise attributed to Lucian[3] says, *she was Nature, the parent of things, or the creatress.* She was therefore the same as Isis, who was the prolific material upon which both the creative and destructive attributes operated.[4] As water was her terrestrial essence, so was the moon her celestial image, whose attractive power, heaving the waters of the ocean, naturally led men to associate them. The moon was

[1] *De Bell oParthico.*
[2] *In Crasso.*
[3] *De Dea Syriâ.*
[4] Plutarch. *de Is. & Os.*

165

also supposed to return the dews which the sun exhaled from the earth; and hence her warmth was reckoned to be moistening, as that of the sun was drying.[1] The Egyptians called her the Mother of the World, because she sowed and scattered into the air the prolific principles with which she had been impregnated by the sun.[2] These principles, as well as the light by which she was illumined, being supposed to emanate from the great fountain of all life and motion, partook of the nature of the being from which they were derived. Hence the Egyptians attributed to the moon, as well as to the sun, the active and passive powers of generation,[3] which were both, to use the languages of the scholastics, *essentially* the same, though *formally* different. This union is represented on a medal of Demetrius the second, king of Syria,[4] where the goddess of Hierapolis appears with the male organs of generation sticking out of her robe, and holding the thyrsus of Bacchus, the emblem of fire, in one hand, and the terrestrial globe, representing the subordinate elements, in the other. Her head is crowned with various plants, and on each side is an asterisc representing (probably) the diur-

[1] *Calor solis arefacit, lunaris humectat.* Macrob. *Sat.* vii. c. 10.
[2] Plutarch. *de Is. & Os.*
[3] Ibid.
[4] Plate x. Fig. 5, from Haym. *Tes. Brit.* p. 70.

nal and nocturnal sun, in the same manner as when placed over the caps of Castor and Pollux.[1] This is not the form under which she was represented in the temple at Hierapolis, when the author of the account attributed to Lucian visited it; which is not to be wondered at, for the figures of this universal goddess, being merely emblematical, were composed according to the attributes which the artists meant particularly to express. She is probably represented here in the form under which she was worshipped in the neighbourhood of Cyzicus, where she was called Αρτεμις Πριαπινη, the *Priapic Diana.*[2] In the temple at Hierapolis the active powers imparted to her by the Creator were represented by immense images of the male organs of generation placed on each side of the door. The measures of these must necessarily be corrupt in the present text of Lucian; but that they were of an enormous size we may conclude from what is related of a man's going to the top of one of them every year, and residing there seven days, in order to have a more intimate communication with the deity, while praying for the prosperity of Syria.[3] Athenæus relates, that Ptolemy Philadelphus had one of 120 cubits long carried in

[1] See Plate ix. Fig. 7.
[2] Plutarch. *in Lucullo.*
[3] Lucian. *de Dea Syriâ.*

procession at Alexandria,[1] of which the poet might justly have said—

> Horrendum protendit Mentula contum
> Quanta queat vastos Thetidis spumantis hiatus;
> Quanta queat priscamque Rheam, magnamque parentem
> Naturam, solidis naturam implere medullis,
> Si foret immensos, quot ad astra volantia currunt,
> Conceptura globos, et tela trisulca tonantis,
> Et vaga concussum motura tonitrua mundum.

This was the real meaning of the enormous figures at Hierapolis:—they were the generative organs of the creator personified, with which he was supposed to have impregnated the heavens, the earth, and the waters. Within the temple were many small statues of men with these organs disproportionably large. These were the angels or attendants of the goddess, who acted as her ministers of creation in peopling and fructifying the earth. The statue of the goddess herself was in the sanctuary of the temple; and near it was the statue of the creator, whom the author calls Jupiter, as he does the goddess, Juno; by which he only means that they were the supreme deities of the country where worshipped. She was borne by lions, and he by bulls, to show that nature, the passive productive power of matter, was sustained by anterior destruction, whilst the ætherial spirit, or active productive power, was sustained by his own

[1] *Deipnos. lib.*

strength only, of which the bulls were symbols.[1] Between both was a third figure, with a dove on his head, which some thought to be Bacchus.[2] This was the Holy Spirit, the first-begotten love, or plastic nature, (of which the dove was the image when it really deigned to descend upon man,[3]) proceeding from, and consubstantial with *both;* for all *three* were but personifications of *one.* The dove, or some fowl like it, appears on the medals of Gortyna in Crete, acting the same part with Dictynna, the Cretan Diana, as the swan is usually represented acting with Leda.[4] This composition has nearly the same signification as that before described of the bull in the lap of Ceres, Diana being equally a personification of the productive power of the earth. It may seem extraordinary, that after this adventure with the dove, she should still remain a virgin; but mysteries of this kind are to be found in all religions. Juno is said to have renewed her virginity every year by bathing

---

[1] The *active* and *passive* powers of creation are called *male* and *female* by the Ammonian Platonics. See Proclus *in Theol. Platon.* lib. 1. c. 28.

[2] Lucian, *de Dea Syriâ.*

[3] Matth. ch. iii. ver. 17.

[4] See Plate III. Fig. 5. Καλψοι δε την Αρτεμιν Θραχες Βενδειαν, Κρητες δε Διχτυνναν. Palæph. *de Incred.* Tab. xxxi. See also Diodor. Sic. lib. v. & Euripid. *Hippol.* v. 145.

in a certain fountain;[1] a miracle which I believe even modern legends cannot parallel.

In the vision of Ezekiel, God is described as descending upon the combined forms of the eagle, the bull, and the lion,[2] the emblems of the ætherial spirit, the creative and destructive powers, which were all united in the true God, though hypostatically divided in the Syrian trinity. Man was compounded with them, as representing the real image of God, according to the Jewish theology. The cherubim on the ark of the covenant, between which God dwelt,[3] were also compounded of the same forms,[4] so that the idea of them must have been present to the prophet's mind, previous to the apparition which furnished him with the description. Even those on the ark of the covenant, though made at the express command of God, do not appear to have been original; for a figure exactly answering to the description of them appears among those curious ruins existing at Chilminar, in Persia, which have been supposed to be those of the palace of Persepolis, burnt by Alexander; but for what reason, it is not easy to conjecture. They do not, certainly, answer to any ancient

---

[1] Pausan. lib. ii. c. 38.
[2] Ezek. ch. i. ver. 10, with Lowth's *Comm.*
[3] *Exod.* ch. xxv. ver. 22.
[4] Spencer *de Leg. Ritual Vet. Hebræor*, lib. iii. dissert. 5.

Fig. 1.

Fig. 2.

Fig. 4.

Fig. 7.

Fig. 5.

Fig. 3.

Fig. 6.

PLATE XXI

BACCHUS AND MEDALS OF CAMARINA AND SYRACUSE

description extant of that celebrated palace; but, as far as we can judge of them in their present state, appear evidently to have been a temple.[1] But the Persians, as before observed, had no inclosed temples or statues, which they held in such abhorrence, that they tried every means possible to destroy those of the Egyptians; thinking it unworthy of the majesty of the deity to have his all-pervading presence limited to the boundary of an edifice, or likened to an image of stone or metal. Yet, among the ruins at Chilminar, we not only find many statues, which are evidently of ideal beings,[2] but also that remarkable emblem of the deity, which distinguishes almost all the Egyptian temples now extant.[3] The portals are also of the same form as those at Thebes and Philæ; and, except the hieroglyphics which distinguish the latter, are finished and ornamented nearly in the same manner. Unless, therefore, we suppose the Persians to have been so inconsistent as to erect temples in direct contradiction to the first principles of their own religion, and decorate them with sym-

[1] See Le Bruyn, *Voyage en Perse*, Planche cxxiii.
[2] See Le Bruyn and Niebuhr.
[3] See Plate xviii. Fig. 1 from the Isiac Table, and Plate xix. Fig 5 from Niebuhr's prints of Chilminar. See also Plate xviii. Fig. 2 and Plate xix. Fig. i from the Isiac Tables and the Egyptian Portals published by Norden and Pococke, on every one of which this singular emblem occurs.

bols and images, which they held to be impious and abominable, we cannot suppose them to be the authors of these buildings. Neither can we suppose the Parthians, or later Persians, to have been the builders of them; for both the style of workmanship in the figures, and the forms of the letters in the inscriptions, denote a much higher antiquity, as will appear evidently to any one who will take the trouble of comparing the drawings published by Le Bruyn and Niebuhr with the coins of the Arsacidæ and Sassanidæ. Almost all the symbolical figures are to be found repeated upon different Phœnician coins; but the letters of the Phœnicians, which are said to have come to them from the Assyrians, are much less simple, and evidently belong to an alphabet much further advanced in improvement. Some of the figures are also observable upon the Greek coins, particularly the bull and lion fighting, and the mystic flower, which is the constant device of the Rhodians. The style of workmanship is also exactly the same as that of the very ancient Greek coins of Acanthus, Celendaris, and Lesbos; the lines being very strongly marked, and the hair expressed by round knobs. The wings likewise of the figure, which resembles the Jewish cherubim, are the same as those upon several Greek sculptures now extant; such as the little images of Priapus attached to the ancient bracelets,

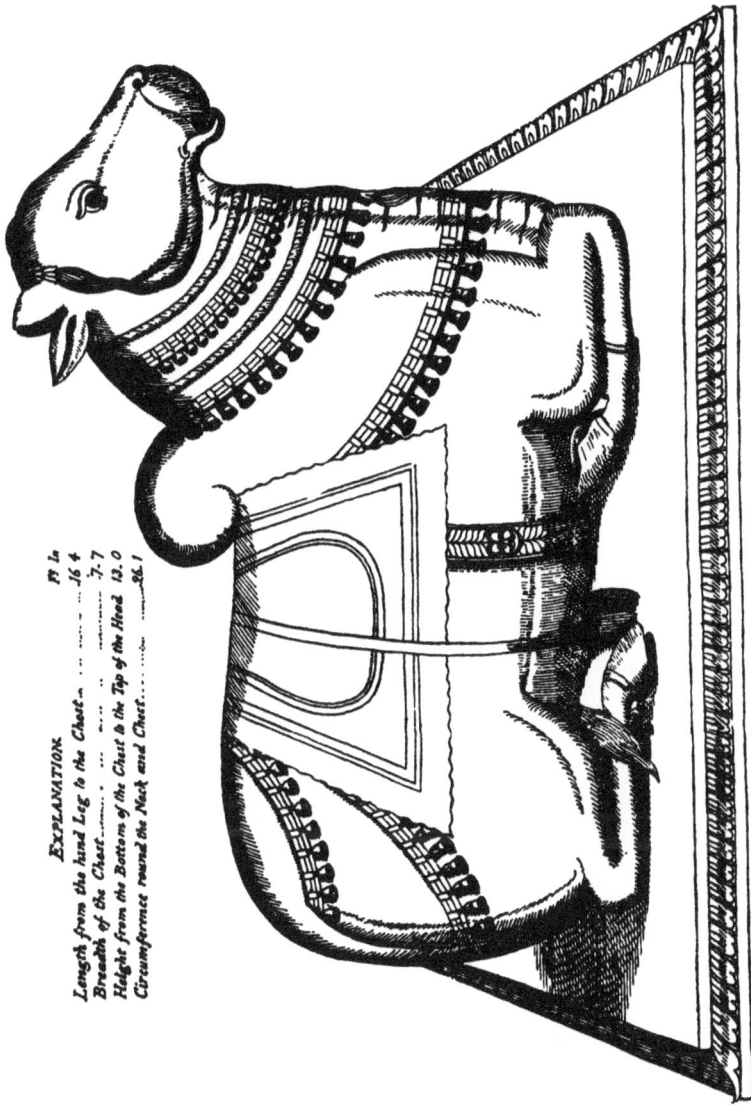

EXPLANATION

Length from the hind Leg to the Chest 16 4

Breadth of the Chest 7. 7

Height from the Bottom of the Chest to the Top of the Head 12. 0

Circumference round the Neck and Chest 26. 1

Statue of a Bull in the Pagoda of Tanjore.

PLATE XXII

the compound figures of the goat and lion upon the frieze of the Temple of Apollo Didymæus, &c. &c.[1] They are likewise joined to the human figure on the medals of Melita and Camarina,[2] as well as upon many ancient sculptures in relief found in Persia.[3] The feathers in these wings are turned upwards like those of an ostrich,[4] to which however they have no resemblance in form, but seem rather like those of a fowl brooding, though more distorted than any I ever observed in nature. Whether this distortion was meant to express lust or incubation, I cannot determine; but the compositions, to which the wings are added, leave little doubt, that it was meant for the one or the other. I am inclined to believe that it was for the latter, as we find on the medals of Melita a figure with four of these wings, who seems by his attitude to be brooding over something.[5] On his head is the cap of liberty, whilst in his right hand he holds the hook or attractor, and in his left the winnow or separator; so that he probably represents the Ερως, or generative spirit brooding over matter, and giving

[1] See Le Bruyn, Planche cxxiii. *Ionian Antiquities*, vol. 1. c. 3. Plate ix., and Plate ii. Fig. 2.

[2] See Plate xx. Fig. 2, from one of Melita, belonging to me.

[3] See Le Bruyn, Planche cxxi.

[4] As those on Figures described by Ezekiel were. See c. i. v. ii.

[5] See Plate xx. Fig. 2, engraved from one belonging to me.

liberty to its productive powers by the exertion of his own attributes, attraction and separation. On a very ancient Phœnician medal brought from Asia by Mr. Pullinger, and published very incorrectly by Mr. Swinton in the Philosophical Transactions of 1760, is a disc or ring surrounded by wings of different forms, of which some of the feathers are distorted in the same manner.[1] The same disc, surrounded by the same kind of wings, incloses the asterisc of the sun over the bull Apis, or Mnevis, on the Isiac Table,[2] where it also appears with many of the other Egyptian symbols, particularly over the heads of Isis and Osiris.[3] It is also placed over the entrances of most of the Egyptian temples described by Pococke and Norden as well as on that represented on the Isiac Table,[4] though with several variations, and without the asterisc. We find it equally without the asterisc, but with little or no variation, on the ruins at Chilmenar, and other supposed Persian antiquities in that neighbourhood:[5] but upon some of the Greek medals the asterisc alone is placed over the bull with

[1] See Plate IX. Fig. 9, engraved from the original medal, now belonging to me.

[2] See Plate XIX, Fig. 1, from Pignorius.

[3] See Plate XVIII. Fig. 2, from Pignorius.

[4] See Plate XVIII. Fig. 1, from Pignorius.

[5] See Niebuhr and Le Bruyn, and Plate XIX. Fig. 2, from the former.

the human face,[1] who is then the same as the Apis or
Mnevis of the Egyptians; that is, the image of the
generative power of the sun, which is signified by
the asterisc on the Greek medals, and by the kneph,
or winged disc, on the Oriental monuments. The
Greeks however sometimes employed this latter symbol, but contrived, according to their usual practice,
to join it to the human figure, as may be seen on a
medal of Camarina, published by Prince Torrem-
muzzi.[2] On other medals of this city the same idea
is expressed, without the disc or asterisc, by a winged
figure, which appears hovering over a swan, the
emblem of the waters, to show the generative power
of the sun fructifying that element, or adding the
active to the *passive* powers of production.[3] On the
medals of Naples, a winged figure of the same kind
is represented crowning the Taurine Bacchus with a
wreath of laurel.[4] This antiquarians have called a
Victory crowning the Minotaur; but the fabulous
monster called the Minotaur was never said to have
been victorious, even by the poets who invented it;
and whenever the sculptors and painters represented

[1] See Plate IV. Fig. 2, and Plate XIX. Fig. 4, from a medal of
Cales, belonging to me.
[2] See Plate XXI. Fig. 2, copied from it.
[3] See Plate XXI. Fig. 3, from one belonging to me.
[4] See Plate XIX. Fig. 5. The coins are common in all collections.

it, they joined the head of a bull to a human body, as may be seen in the celebrated picture of Theseus, published among the antiquities of Herculaneum, and on the medals of Athens, struck about the time of Severus, when the style of art was totally changed, and the mystic theology extinct. The winged figure, which has been called a Victory, appears mounting in the chariot of the sun, on the medals of queen Philistis,[1] and, on some of those of Syracuse, flying before it in the place where the asterisc appears on others of the same city.[2] I am therefore persuaded, that these are only different modes of representing one idea, and that the winged figure means the same, when placed over the Taurine Bacchus of the Greeks, as the winged disc over the Apis or Mnevis of the Egyptians. The Ægis, or snaky breastplate, and the Medusa's head, are also, as Dr. Stukeley justly observed,[3] Greek modes of representing this winged disc joined with the serpents, as it frequently is, both in the Egyptian sculptures, and those of Chilmenar in Persia. The expressions of rage and violence, which usually characterise the countenance of Medusa, signify the destroying attribute joined with the generative, as both were equally under the direction of

[1] See Plate xxi. Fig. 4, from one belonging to me.
[2] See Plate xxi. Fig. 5 and 6, from coins belonging to me.
[3] Abury, p. 93.

Minerva, or divine wisdom. I am inclined to believe, that the large rings, to which the little figures of Priapus are attached,[1] had also the same meaning as the disc; for, if intended merely to suspend them by, they are of an extravagant magnitude, and would not answer their purpose so well as a common loop.

On the Phœnician coin above mentioned, this symbol, the winged disc, is placed over a figure sitting, who holds in his hands an arrow, whilst a bow, ready bent, of the ancient Scythian form, lies by him.[2] On his head is a large loose cap, tied under his chin, which I take to be the lion's skin, worn in the same manner as on the heads of Hercules, upon the medals of Alexander; but the work is so small, though executed with extreme nicety and precision, and perfectly preserved, that it is difficult to decide with certainty what it represents, in parts of such minuteness. The bow and arrows, we know, were the ancient arms of Hercules;[3] and continued so, until the Greek poets thought proper to give him the club.[4] He was particularly worshipped at Tyre, the metropolis of Phœnicia;[5] and his head appears in the

[1] See Plate II. Fig. 1, and Plate III. Fig. 2.
[2] See Plate IX. Fig. 10 *b*.
[3] Homer's *Odyss.* Λ, ver. 606.
[4] Strabo, lib. xiv.
[5] Macrob. *Sat.* lib. i. c. 20.

usual form, on many of the coins of that people. We may hence conclude that he is the person here represented, notwithstanding the difference in the style and composition of the figure, which may be accounted for by the difference of art. The Greeks, animated by the spirit of their ancient poets, and the glowing melody of their language, were grand and poetical in all their compositions; whilst the Phœnicians, who spoke a harsh and untuneable dialect, were unacquainted with fine poetry, and consequently with poetical ideas; for words being the types of ideas, and the signs or marks by which men not only communicate them to each other, but arrange and regulate them in their own minds, the genius of a language goes a great way towards forming the character of the people who use it. Poverty of expression will produce poverty of conception; for men will never be able to form sublime ideas, when the language in which they *think* (for men always think as well as speak in some language) is incapable of expressing them. This may be one reason why the Phœnicians never rivalled the Greeks in the perfection of art, although they attained a degree of excellence long before them; for Homer, whenever he has occasion to speak of any fine piece of art, takes care to inform us that it was the work of Sidonians. He also mentions the Phœnician merchants bringing toys and ornaments of dress to sell to the Greeks, and practicing those frauds which merchants and factors are apt to practice upon ignorant people.[1] It is probable that their progress in the fine arts, like that of the Dutch (who are the Phœnicians of modern history), never went beyond a strict imitation of nature; which, compared to the more elevated graces of ideal composition, is like a newspaper narrative compared with one of Homer's battles. A figure of Hercules, therefore, executed by a Phœnician artist, if compared to one by Phidias or Lysippus, would be like a picture of Moses or David, painted by Teniers, or Gerard Dow, compared to one of the same, painted by Raphael or Annibal Caracci. This is exactly the difference between the figures on the medal now under consideration, and those on the coins of Gelo or Alexander. Of all the personages of the ancient mythology, Hercules is perhaps the most difficult to explain; for physical allegory and fabulous history are so entangled in the accounts we have of him, that it is scarcely possible to separate them. He appears however, like all the other gods, to have been originally a personified attribute of the sun. The eleventh of the Orphic Hymns [2] is addressed to

[1] Homer. *Odyss. 0,* ver. 414.
[2] *Ed. Gesner.*

him as the strength and power of the sun; and Macrobius says that he was thought to be the strength and virtue of the gods, by which they destroyed the giants; and that, according to Varro, the Mars and Hercules of the Romans were the same deity, and worshipped with the same rites.[1] According to Varro then, whose authority is perhaps the greatest that can be cited, Hercules was the destroying attribute represented in a human form, instead of that of a lion, tiger, or hippopotamus. Hence the terrible picture drawn of him by Homer, which always appeared to me to have been taken from some symbolical statue, which the poet not understanding, supposed to be of the Theban hero, who had assumed the title of the deity, and whose fabulous history he was well acquainted with. The description however applies in every particular to the allegorical personage. His attitude, ever fixed in the act of letting fly his arrow,[2] with the figures of lions and bears, battles and murders, which adorn his belt, all unite in representing him as the destructive attribute personified. But how happens it then that he is so frequently represented strangling the lion, the natural emblem of this power? Is this an historical fable belonging to the

[1] *Sat.* lib. 1. c. 20.

[2] Αιει Βαλεοντι ἐοικως. *Odyss.* λ, ver. 607.

Theban hero, or a physical allegory of the destructive power destroying its own force by its own exertions? Or is the single attribute personified taken for the whole power of the deity in this, as in other instances already mentioned? The Orphic Hymn above cited seems to favour this last conjecture; for he is there addressed both as the devourer and generator of all (Παμφαγε, παγγενετωζ). However this may be, we may safely conclude that the Hercules armed with the bow and arrow, as he appears on the present medal, is like the Apollo, the destroying power of the diurnal sun.

On the other side of the medal [1] is a figure, somewhat like the Jupiter on the medals of Alexander and Antiochus, sitting with a beaded sceptre in his right hand, which he rests upon the head of a bull, that projects from the side of the chair. Above, on his right shoulder, is a bird, probably a dove, the symbol of the Holy Spirit, descending from the sun, but, as this part of the medal is less perfect than the rest, the species cannot be clearly discovered. In his left hand he holds a short staff, from the upper side of which springs an ear of corn, and from the lower a bunch of grapes, which being the two most esteemed productions of the earth, were the natural emblems

[1] See Plate IX. Fig. 10 *a*.

of general fertilization. This figure is therefore the generator, as that on the other side is the destroyer, whilst the sun, of whose attributes both are personifications, is placed between them. The letters on the side of the generator are quite entire, and, according to the Phœnician alphabet published by Mr. Dutens, are equivalent to the Roman ones which compose the words *Baal Thrz*, of which Mr. Swinton makes *Baal Tarz*, and translates *Jupiter of Tarsus;* whence he concludes that this coin was struck at that city. But the first letter of the last word is not a *Teth*, but a *Thau*, or aspirated T; and, as the Phœnicians had a vowel answering to the Roman A, it is probable they would have inserted it, had they intended it to be sounded: but we have no reason to believe that they had any to express the U or Y, which must therefore be comprehended in the preceding consonant whenever the sound is expressed. Hence I conclude that the word here meant is *Thyrz* or *Thurz*, the *Thor* or *Thur* of the Celtes and Sarmatians, the *Thurra* of the Assyrians, the *Turan* of the Tyrrhenians or Etruscans, the *Taurine Bacchus* of the Greeks, and the deity whom the Germans carried with them in the shape of a bull, when they invaded Italy; from whom the city of Tyre, as well as Tyrrhenia, or Tuscany, probably took its name. His symbol the bull, to which the name alludes, is represented on the chair or

throne in which he sits; and his sceptre, the emblem
of his authority, rests upon it. The other word, *Baal,*
was merely a title in the Phœnician language, signifying *God, or Lord;*[1] and used as án epithet of the
sun, as we learn from the name Baal-bec (*the city
of Baal*), which the Greeks rendered Heliopolis (*the
city of the sun*).

Thus does this singular medal show the fundamental principles of the ancient Phœnician religion
to be the same as those which appear to have prevailed through all the other nations of the northern
hemisphere. Fragments of the same system every
where occur, variously expressed as they were variously understood, and oftentimes merely preserved
without being understood at all; the ancient reverence being continued to the symbols, when their
meaning was wholly forgotten. The *hypostatical* division and *essential* unity of the deity is one of the
most remarkable parts of this system, and the far-
thest removed from common sense and reason; and
yet this is perfectly reasonable and consistent, if
considered together with the rest of it: for the emanations and personifications were only figurative ab-
stractions of particular modes of action and existence,
of which the primary cause and original essence still
continued one and the same

[1] *Cleric. Comm. in 2 Reg. c. i. ver. 2.*

The three hypostases being thus only one being, each hypostasis is occasionally taken for all; as is the case in the passage of Apuleius before cited, where Isis describes herself as the universal deity. In this character she is represented by a small basaltine figure, of Egyptian sculpture, at Strawberry Hill, which is covered over with symbols of various kinds from top to bottom.[1] That of the bull is placed lowest, to show that the strength or power of the creator is the foundation and support of every other attribute. On her head are towers, to denote the earth; and round her neck is hung a crab-fish, which, from its power of spontaneously detaching from its body, and naturally reproducing, any limbs that are hurt or mutilated, became the symbol of the productive power of the waters; in which sense it appears on great numbers of ancient medals of various cities.[2] The nutritive power is signified by her many breasts, and the destructive by the lions which she bears on her arms. Other attributes are expressed by various

---

[1] A print of one exactly the same is published by Montfaucon, *Antiq. expliq.* vol. i. Plate xciii. Fig. i.

[2] See those of Agrigentum, Himera, and Cyrene. On a small one of the first-mentioned city, belonging to me, a cross, the abbreviated symbol of the male powers of generation, approaches the mouth of the crab, while the cornucopia issues from it (see Plate xx. Fig. 3): the one represents the cause, and the other the effect of fertilization.

other animal symbols, the precise meaning of which I have not sagacity sufficient to discover.

This universality of the goddess was more concisely represented in other figures of her, by the mystic instrument called a *Systrum*, which she carried in her hand. Plutarch has given an explanation of it,[1] which may serve to show that the mode here adopted of explaining the ancient symbols is not founded merely upon conjecture and analogy, but also upon the authority of one of the most grave and learned of the Greeks. The curved top, he says, represented the lunar orbit, within which the creative attributes of the deity were exerted, in giving motion to the four elements, signified by the four rattles below.[2] On the centre of the curve was a cat, the emblem of the moon; who, from her influence on the constitutions of women, was supposed to preside particularly over the passive powers of generation;[3] and below, upon the base, a head of Isis or Nepthus; instead of which, upon that which I have had engraved, as well as upon many others now extant, are the male organs of generation, representing the active powers of the creator, attributed to Isis with the

[1] *De Is. & Os.*

[2] See Plate x. Fig. 4, engraved from one in the collection of R. Wilbraham, Esq.

[3] Cic. *de Nat. Deor.* lib. ii. c. 46.

passive. The clattering noise, and various motions of the rattles being adopted as the symbols of the movement and mixture of the elements from which all things are produced; the sound of metals in general became an emblem of the same kind. Hence, the ringing of bells, and clattering of plates of metal, were used in all lustrations, sacrifices, &c.[1] The title Priapus, applied to the characteristic attribute of the creator, and sometimes to the Creator himself, is probably a corruption of Βριαπυοε (clamorous or loud); for the B and Π being both labials, the change of the one for the other is common in the Greek language. We still find many ancient images of this symbol, with bells attached to them,[2] as they were to the sacred robe of the high priest of the Jews, in which he administered to the Creator.[3] The bells in both were of a pyramidal form,[4] to shew the ætherial igneous essence of the god. This form is still retained in those used in our churches, as well as in the little ones rung by the Catholic priests at the elevation of the host. The use of them was early adopted by the Christians, in the same sense as they were employed

---

[1] Clem. Alex. Προτζ. p. 9. *Schol in Theocrit.* Idyll. ||. ver. 36.
[2] *Bronzi dell' Hercol. Tom.* vi. Plate xcviii.
[3] *Exod.* ch. xxviii.
[4] Bronzi dell' Hercol. Tom. vi. Plate xcviii. Maimonides in Patrick's *Commentary on Exodus*, ch. xxviii.

by the later heathens; that is, as a charm against evil
dæmons; [1] for, being symbols of the active exertions
of the creative attributes, they were properly op-
posed to the emanations of the destructive. The Lace-
demonians used to beat a pan or kettle-drum at the
death of their king, [2] to assist in the emancipation of
his soul at the dissolution of the body. We have a
similar custom of tolling a bell on such occasions,
which is very generally practised, though the meaning of it has been long forgotten. This emancipation
of the soul was supposed to be finally performed by
fire; which, being the visible image and active essence of both the creative and destructive powers,
was very naturally thought to be the medium through
which men passed from the present to a future life.
The Greeks, and all the Celtic nations, accordingly,
burned the bodies of the dead, as the Gentoos do at
this day; while the Egyptians, among whom fuel was
extremely scarce, placed them in pyramidal monuments, which were the symbols of fire; hence come
those prodigious structures which still adorn that
country. The soul which was to be emancipated
was the divine emanation, the vital spark of heavenly
flame, the principle of reason and perception, which

[1] Ovid. *Fast.* lib. v. ver. 441. *Schol. in* Theocrit Idyll. ii.
ver. 36.

[2] *Schol. in* Theocrit. Idyll. ii. ver. 36.

was personified into the familiar dæmon, or genius, supposed to have the direction of each individual, and to dispose him to good or evil, wisdom or folly, and all their consequences of prosperity and adversity.[1] Hence proceeded the doctrines, so uniformly inculcated by Homer and Pindar,[2] of all human actions depending immediately upon the gods; which were adopted, with scarcely any variations, by some of the Christian divines of the apostolic age. In the Pastor of Hermas, and Recognitions of Clemens, we find the angels of justice, penitence, and sorrow, instead of the genii, or dæmons, which the ancients supposed to direct men's minds and inspire them with those particular sentiments. St. Paul adopted the still more comfortable doctrine of grace, which served full as well to emancipate the consciences of the faithful from the shackles of practical morality. The familiar dæmons, or divine emanations, were supposed to reside in the blood; which was thought to contain the principles of vital heat, and was therefore forbidden by Moses.[3] Homer, who seems to have

---

[1] Pindar. *Pyth.* v. ver. 164. Sophocl. *Trachin.* ver. 922. Hor. lib. ii. epist. ii. ver. 187.

[2] Εκ Θεων μαχαναι ηγσαι Βροτεαις αρεταις, και σοφοι, και χερσι Βιαται, περιγλωσσοι τ' εφιν. Pindar *Pyth.* i. ver. 79 Passages to the same purpose occur in almost every page of the *Iliad* and *Odyssey.*

[3] *Levit.* ch. xvii. ver. 11 & 14.

collected little fragments of the ancient theology, and introduced them here and there, amidst the wild profusion of his poetical fables, represents the shades of the deceased as void of perception, until they had tasted of the blood of the victims offered by Ulysses; [1] by which their faculties were renewed by a reunion with the divine emanation, from which they had been separated. The soul of Tiresias is said to be entire in hell, and to possess alone the power of perception, because with him this divine emanation still remained. The shade of Hercules is described among the other ghosts, though he himself, as the poet says, was then in heaven; that is, the active principle of thought and perception returned to its native heaven, whilst the passive, or merely sensitive, remained on earth, from whence it sprung.[2] The final separation of these two did not take place till the body was consumed by fire, as appears from the ghost of Elpenor, whose body being still entire, he retained both, and knew Ulysses before he had tasted of the blood. It was from producing this separation, that the universal Bacchus, or double Apollo, the creator and destroyer, whose essence was fire, was

[1] *Odyss.* ζ, ver. 152.

[2] Those who wish to see the difference between sensation and perception clearly and fully explained, may be satisfied by reading the *Essai analytique sur l'Ame*, by Mr. Bonnet.

also called Λικνιτης, the purifier,[1] by a metaphor taken from the winnow, which purified the corn from the dust and chaff, as fire purified the soul from its terrestrial pollutions. Hence this instrument is called by Virgil the mystic winnow of Bacchus.[2] The Ammonian Platonics and Gnostic Christians thought that this separation, or purification, might be effected in a degree even before death. It was for this purpose that they practised such rigid temperance, and gave themselves up to such intense study; for, by subduing and extenuating the terrestrial principle, they hoped to give liberty and vigour to the celestial, so that it might be enabled to ascend directly to the intellectual world, pure and unincumbered.[3] The clergy afterwards introduced Purgatory, instead of abstract meditation and study; which was the ancient mode of separation by fire, removed into an unknown country, where it was saleable to all such of the inhabitants of this world as had sufficient wealth and credulity.

It was the celestial or ætherial principle of the human mind, which the ancient artists represented under the symbol of the butterfly, which may be

---

[1] *Orph. Hymn.* 45.

[2] *Mystica vannus Iacchi.* Georg. i. ver. 166.

[3] Plotin. *Ennead.* vi. lib. iv. ch. 16. Mosheim, *Not y in* Cudw. *Syst. Intell.* ch. v. sect. 20.

considered as one of the most elegant allegories of their elegant religion. This insect, when hatched from the egg, appears in the shape of a grub, crawling upon the earth, and feeding upon the leaves of plants. In this state, it was aptly made the emblem of man, in his earthly form, in which the ætherial vigour and activity of the celestial soul, the *divine particula mentis,* was supposed to be clogged and incumbered with the material body. When the grub was changed to a chrysalis, its stillness, torpor, and insensibility seemed to present a natural image of death, or the intermediate state between the cessation of the vital functions of the body and the final releasement of the soul by the fire, in which the body was consumed. The butterfly breaking from the torpid chrysalis, and mounting in the air, was no less natural an image of the celestial soul bursting from the restraints of matter, and mixing again with its native æther. The Greek artists, always studious of elegance, changed this, as well as other animal symbols, into a human form, retaining the wings as the characteristic members, by which the meaning might be known. The human body, which they added to them, is that of a beautiful girl, sometimes in the age of infancy, and sometimes of approaching maturity. So beautiful an allegory as this would naturally be a favourite subject of art among a people whose taste had attained the utmost pitch of refinement. We accordingly find that it has been more frequently and more variously repeated than any other which the system of emanations, so favourable to art, could afford.

Although all men were supposed to partake of the divine emanation in a degree, it was not supposed that they all partook of it in an equal degree. Those who showed superior abilities, and distinguished themselves by their splendid actions, were supposed to have a larger share of the divine essence, and were therefore adored as gods, and honoured with divine titles, expressive of that particular attribute of the deity with which they seemed to be most favoured. New personages were thus enrolled among the allegorical deities; and the personified attributes of the sun were confounded with a Cretan and Thessalian king, an Asiatic conqueror, and a Theban robber. Hence Pindar, who appears to have been a very orthodox heathen, says, that the race of men and gods is one, that both breathe from one mother, and only differ in power.[1] This confusion of epithets and titles contributed, as much as any thing, to raise that vast and extravagant fabric of poetical mythology, which, in a manner, overwhelmed the ancient the-

[1] *Nem.* v. ver. i.

ology, which was too pure and philosophical to continue long a popular religion. The grand and exalted system of a general first cause, universally expanded, did not suit the gross conceptions of the multitude; who had no other way of conceiving the idea of an omnipotent god, but by forming an exaggerated image of their own despot, and supposing his power to consist in an unlimited gratification of his passions and appetites. Hence the universal Jupiter, the aweful and venerable, the general principle of life and motion, was transformed into the god who thundered from Mount Ida, and was lulled to sleep in the embraces of his wife; and hence the god whose spirit moved [1] upon the face of the waters, and impregnated them with the powers of generation, became a great king above all gods, who led forth his people to smite the ungodly, and rooted out their enemies from before them.

Another great means of corrupting the ancient theology, and establishing the poetical mythology, was the practice of the artists in representing the various attributes of the creator under human forms of various character and expression. These figures, being

[1] So the translators have rendered the expression of the original, which literally means brooding as a fowl on its eggs, and alludes to the symbols of the ancient theology, which I have before observed upon. See Patrick's *Commentary*.

distinguished by the titles of the deity which they were meant to represent, became in time to be considered as distinct personages, and worshipped as separate subordinate deities. Hence the many-shaped god, the πολυμορφος and μυριομορφος of the ancient theologists, became divided into many gods and goddesses, often described by the poets as at variance with each other and wrangling about the little intrigues and passions of men. Hence too, as the symbols were multiplied, particular ones lost their dignity; and that venerable one which is the subject of this discourse, became degraded from the representative of the god of nature to a subordinate rural deity, a supposed son of the Asiatic conqueror Bacchus, standing among the nymphs by a fountain,[1] and expressing the fertility of a garden, instead of the general creative power of the great active principle of the universe. His degradation did not stop even here; for we find him, in times still more prophane and corrupt, made a subject of raillery and insult, as answering no better purpose than holding up his rubicund snout to frighten the birds and thieves.[2] His talents were also perverted from their natural ends, and employed in base and abortive efforts in con-

---

[1] Theocrit. Idyll. 1. ver. 21.
[2] Horat. lib. 1. Sat. viii. Virg. *Georg.* iv.

formity to the taste of the times; for men naturally attribute their own passions and inclinations to the objects of their adoration; and as God made man in his own image, so man returns the favour, and makes God in his. Hence we find the highest attribute of the all-pervading spirit and first-begotten love foully prostituted to promiscuous vice, and calling out, *Hæc cunnum, caput hic, præbeat ille nates.*[1]

He continued however still to have his temple, priestess and sacred geese,[2] and offerings of the most exquisite kind were made to him:

> Crissabitque tibi excussis pulcherrima lumbis
> Hoc anno primum experta puella virum.

Sometimes, however, they were not so scrupulous in the selection of their victims, but suffered frugality to restrain their devotion:

> Cum sacrum fieret Deo salaci
> Conducta est pretio puella parvo.[3]

The bride was usually placed upon him immediately before marriage; not, as Lactantius says, *ut ejus pudicitiam prior Deus prælibasse videatur,* but that she might be rendered fruitful by her communion with the divine nature, and capable of fulfilling the

[1] Priap. Carm. 21.
[2] Petron. *Satyric.*
[3] Priap. Carm. 34.

duties of her station. In an ancient poem [1] we find a lady of the name of Lalage presenting the pictures of the "Elephantis" to him, and gravely requesting that she might enjoy the pleasures over which he particularly presided, in all the attitudes described in that celebrated treatise.[2] Whether or not she succeeded, the poet has not informed us; but we may safely conclude that she did not trust wholly to faith and prayer, but, contrary to the usual practice of modern devotees, accompanied her devotion with such good works as were likely to contribute to the end proposed by it.

When a lady had served as the victim in a sacrifice to this god, she expressed her gratitude for the benefits received, by offering upon his altar certain small images representing his characteristic attribute, the number of which was equal to the number of men who had acted as priests upon the occasion.[3] On an antique gem, in the collection of Mr. Townley, is one of these fair victims, who appears just returned from a sacrifice of this kind, and devoutly returning her thanks by offering upon an altar some of these images, from the number of which one may observe

[1] Priap. Carm. 3.

[2] The *Elephantis* was written by one Philænis, and seems to have been of the same kind with the *Puttana errante* of Aretin.

[3] Priap. Carm. 34. *Ed. Scioppii.*

that she has not been neglected.[1] This offering of thanks had also its mystic and allegorical meaning; for fire being the energetic principle and essential force of the Creator, and the symbol above mentioned the visible image of his characteristic attribute, the uniting them was uniting the material with the essential cause, from whose joint operation all things were supposed to proceed.

These sacrifices, as well as all those to the deities presiding over generation, were performed by night: hence Hippolytus, in Euripides, says, to express his love of chastity, that he likes none of the gods revered by night.[2] These acts of devotion were indeed attended with such rites as must naturally shock the prejudices of a chaste and temperate mind, not liable to be warmed by that ecstatic enthusiasm which is peculiar to devout persons when their attention is absorbed in the contemplation of the beneficent powers of the Creator, and all their faculties directed to imitate him in the exertion of his great characteristic attribute. To heighten this enthusiasm, the male and female saints of antiquity used to lie promiscuously together in the temples, and honour God by a liberal display and general communication of his bounties.[3]

[1] See Plate III. Fig. 3.
[2] Ver. 613.
[3] Herodot. lib. ii.

Herodotus, indeed, excepts the Greeks and Egyptians, and Dionysius of Halicarnassus, the Romans, from this general custom of other nations; but to the testimony of the former we may oppose the thousand sacred prostitutes kept at each of the temples of Corinth and Eryx; [1] and to that of the latter the express words of Juvenal, who, though he lived an age, later, lived when the same religion, and nearly the same manners, prevailed. [2] Diodorus Siculus also tells us, that when the Roman prætors visited Eryx, they laid aside their magisterial severity, and honoured the goddess by mixing with her votaries, and indulging themselves in the pleasures over which she presided. [3] It appears, too, that the act of generation was a sort of sacrament in the island of Lesbos; for the device on its medals (which in the Greek republics had always some relation to religion) is as explicit as forms can make it. [4] The figures appear indeed to be mystic and allegorical, the male having evidently a mixture of the goat in his beard and features, and therefore probably represents Pan, the generative power of the universe incorporated in universal matter. The female has all that breadth and

[1] Strab. lib. viii.
[2] *Sat.* ix. ver. 24.
[3] Lib. iv. *Ed. Wessel.*
[4] See Plate ix. Fig. 8, from one belonging to me.

fulness which characterise the personification of the passive power, known by the titles of Rhea, Juno, Ceres, &c.

When there were such seminaries for female education as those of Eryx and Corinth, we need not wonder that the ladies of antiquity should be extremely well instructed in all the practical duties of their religion. The stories told of Julia and Messalina show us that the Roman ladies were no ways deficient; and yet they were as remarkable for their gravity and decency as the Corinthians were for their skill and dexterity in adapting themselves to all the modes and attitudes which the luxuriant imaginations of experienced votaries have contrived for performing the rites of their tutelar goddess.[1]

The reason why these rites were always performed by night was the peculiar sanctity attributed to it by the ancients, because dreams were then supposed to descend from heaven to instruct and forewarn men. The nights, says Hesiod, belong to the blessed gods; [2] and the Orphic poet calls night the source of all things (παντων γενεσις) to denote that productive power, which, as I have been told, it really possesses; it being observed that plants and animals grow more

[1] Philodemi *Epigr. Brunk. Analect.* vol. ii. p. 85.

[2] Εϱγ· ver. 730.

by night than by day. The ancients extended this power much further, and supposed that not only the productions of the earth, but the luminaries of heaven, were nourished and sustained by the benign influence of the night. Hence that beautiful apostrophe in the "Electra" of Euripides, Ω νυξ μελαινα, χυσεων αστρων τροφε, &c.

Not only the sacrifices to the generative deities, but in general all the religious rites of the Greeks, were of the festive kind. To imitate the gods, was, in their opinion, to feast and rejoice, and to cultivate the useful and elegant arts, by which we are made partakers of their felicity.[1] This was the case with almost all the nations of antiquity, except the [2] Egyptians and their reformed imitators the Jews,[3] who being governed by a hierarchy, endeavoured to make it awful and venerable to the people by an appearance of rigour and austerity. The people, however, sometimes broke through this restraint, and indulged themselves in the more pleasing worship of their neighbours, as when they danced and feasted before the golden calf which Aaron erected,[4] and devoted themselves to the worship of obscene idols, generally

[1] Strabo, lib. x.
[2] Herodot. lib. ii.
[3] See Spencer *de Leg. Rit. Vet. Hebræor.*
[4] *Exod.* ch. xxxii.

supposed to be of Priapus, under the reign of Abijam.[1]

The Christian religion, being a reformation of the Jewish, rather increased than diminished the austerity of its original. On particular occasions however it equally abated its rigour, and gave way to festivity and mirth, though always with an air of sanctity and solemnity. Such were originally the feasts of the Eucharist, which, as the word expresses, were meetings of joy and gratulation; though, as divines tell us, all of the spiritual kind: but the particular manner in which St. Augustine commands the ladies who attended them to wear clean linen,[2] seems to infer, that personal as well as spiritual matters were thought worthy of attention. To those who administer the sacrament in the modern way, it may appear of little consequence whether the women received it in clean linen or not; but to the good bishop, who was to administer the *holy kiss*, it certainly was of some importance. The *holy kiss* was not only applied as a part of the ceremonial of the Eucharist, but also of prayer, at the conclusion of which they welcomed each other with this natural sign of love and benevolence.[3] It was upon these occasions that

[1] *Reg.* c. xv. ver. 13 *Ed. Cleric.*
[2] Aug. *Serm.* clii.
[3] Justin Martyr. *Apolog.*

they worked themselves up to those fits of rapture
and enthusiasm, which made them eagerly rush upon
destruction in the fury of their zeal to obtain the
crown of martyrdom.[1] Enthusiasm on one subject
naturally produces enthusiasm on another; for the
human passions, like the strings of an instrument, vi-
brate to the motions of each other: hence paroxysms
of love and devotion have oftentimes so exactly ac-
corded, as not to have been distinguished by the very
persons whom they agitated.[2] This was too often the
case in these meetings of the primitive Christians.
The feasts of gratulation and love, the αγαπαι and
nocturnal vigils, gave too flattering opportunities to
the passions and appetites of men, to continue long,
what we are told they were at first, pure exercises
of devotion. The spiritual raptures and divine ecstasies encouraged on these occasions, were often
ecstasies of a very different kind, concealed under
the garb of devotion; whence the greatest irregu-
larities ensued; and it became necessary for the repu-
tation of the church, that they should be suppressed,
as they afterwards were by the decrees of several
councils. Their suppression may be considered as
the final subversion of that part of the ancient re-

[1] Martini Kempii *de Osculis Dissert.* viii.
[2] See *Procès de la Cadiere.*

ligion which I have here undertaken to examine; for so long as those nocturnal meetings were preserved, it certainly existed, though under other names, and in a more solemn dress. The small remain of it preserved at Isernia, of which an account has here been given, can scarcely be deemed an exception; for its meaning was unknown to those who celebrated it; and the obscurity of the place, added to the venerable names of S. Cosimo and Damiano, was all that prevented it from being suppressed long ago, as it has been lately, to the great dismay of the chaste matrons and pious monks of Isernia. Traces and memorials of it seem however to have been preserved, in many parts of Christendom, long after the actual celebration of its rites ceased. Hence the obscene figures observable upon many of our Gothic Cathedrals, and particularly upon the ancient brass doors of St. Peter's at Rome, where there are some groups which rival the devices on the Lesbian medals.

It is curious, in looking back through the annals of superstition, so degrading to the pride of man, to trace the progress of the human mind in different ages, climates, and circumstances, uniformly acting upon the same principles, and to the same ends. The sketch here given of the corruptions of the religion of Greece, is an exact counterpart of the history of the corruptions of Christianity, which began in the pure

theism of the eclectic Jews,[1] and by the help of inspi-
rations, emanations, and canonizations, expanded itself, by degrees, to the vast and unwieldly system
which now fills the creed of what is commonly called
the Catholic Church. In the ancient religion, however, the emanations assumed the appearance of
moral virtues and physical attributes, instead of
ministering spirits and guardian angels; and the
canonizations or deifications were bestowed upon
heroes, legislators, and monarchs, instead of priests,
monks, and martyrs. There is also this further difference, that among the moderns philosophy has im-
proved, as religion has been corrupted; whereas,
among the ancients, religion and philosophy declined
together. The true solar system was taught in the
Orphic school, and adopted by the Pythagoreans, the
next regularly-established sect. The Stoics corrupted
it a little, by placing the earth in the centre of the
universe, though they still allowed the sun its superior magnitude.[2] At length arose the Epicureans,
who confounded it entirely, maintaining that the sun
was only a small globe of fire, a few inches in di-

[1] Compare the doctrines of Philo with those taught in the
Gospel of St. John, and Epistles of St. Paul.

[2] Brucker, *Hist. Crit. Philos.* p. ii. lib. ii. c. 9. s. 1.

PLATE XXIII
TIGER AT THE BREAST OF A NYMPH

ameter, and the stars little transitory lights, whirled about in the atmosphere of the earth.[1]

How ill soever adapted the ancient system of emanations was to procure eternal happiness, it was certainly extremely well calculated to produce temporal good; for, by the endless multiplication of subordinate deities, it effectually excluded two of the greatest curses that ever afflicted the human race, dogmatical theology, and its consequent religious persecution. Far from supposing that the gods known in their own country were the only ones existing, the Greeks thought that innumerable emanations of the divine mind were diffused through every part of the universe; so that new objects of devotion presented themselves wherever they went. Every mountain, spring, and river, had its tutelary deity, besides the numbers of immortal spirits that were supposed to wander in the air, scattering dreams and visions, and superintending the affairs of men.

Τρις γαζ μύριοι εισιν επι χθονι πουλύβοτειρη
Αθανατοι Ζηνος, φυλακες θνητων ανθρωπων.[2]

An adequate knowledge of these they never presumed to think attainable, but modestly contented

---

[1] Lucret. lib. v. 565, & seq.

[2] Hesiod. Εργα και Ἡμερ. ver. 252, μυριοι, &c., are always used as the ancient Greek poets.

themselves with revering and invoking them whenever they felt or wanted their assistance. When a
shipwrecked mariner was cast upon an unknown
coast, he immediately offered up his prayers to the
gods of the country, whoever they were; and joined
the inhabitants in whatever rites they thought proper
to propitiate them with.[1] Impious or prophane rites
he never imagined could exist, concluding that all
expressions of gratitude and submission must be
pleasing to the gods. Atheism was, indeed, punished
at Athens, as the obscene ceremonies of the Baccha-
nalians were at Rome; but both as civil crimes
against the state; the one tending to weaken the
bands of society by destroying the sanctity of oaths,
and the other to subvert that decency and gravity of
manners, upon which the Romans so much prided
themselves. The introduction of strange gods, without permission from the magistrate, was also pro-
hibited in both cities; but the restriction extended no
farther than the walls, there being no other parts of
the Roman empire, except Judea, in which any kind
of impiety or extravagance might not have been maintained with impunity, provided it was maintained
merely as a speculative opinion, and not employed as

[1] See Homer. *Odyss.* ε, ver. 445, & seq. The Greeks seem to
have adopted by degrees into their own ritual all the rites practised in the neighbouring countries.

an engine of faction, ambition, or oppression. The
Romans even carried their condescension so far as
to enforce the observance of a dogmatical religion,
where they found it before established; as appears
from the conduct of their magistrates in Judea, relative to Christ and his apostles; and from what
Josephus has related, of a Roman soldier's being
punished with death by his commander for insulting
the Books of Moses. Upon what principle then did
they act, when they afterwards persecuted the Christians with so much rancour and cruelty? Perhaps
it may surprise persons not used to the study of
ecclesiastical antiquities, to be told (what is nevertheless indisputably true) that the Christians were
never persecuted on account of the speculative opinions of individuals, but either for civil crimes laid
to their charge, or for withdrawing their allegiance
from the state, and joining in a federative union
dangerous by its constitution, and rendered still more
dangerous by the intolerant principles of its members, who often tumultuously interrupted the public
worship, and continually railed against the national
religion (with which both the civil government and
military discipline of the Romans were inseparably
connected), as the certain means of eternal damna-
tion. To break this union, was the great object of
Roman policy during a long course of years; but the

violent means employed only tended to cement it closer. Some of the Christians themselves indeed, who were addicted to Platonism, took a safer method to dissolve it; but they were too few in number to succeed. This was by trying to moderate the furious zeal which gave life and vigour to the confederacy, and to blend and soften the unyielding temper of religion with the mild spirit of philosophy. "We all," said they, "agree in worshipping one supreme God, the Father and Preserver of all. While we approach him with purity of mind, sincerity of heart, and innocence of manners, forms and ceremonies of worship are indifferent; and not less worthy of his greatness, for being varied and diversified according to the various customs and opinions of men. Had it been his will that all should have worshipped him in the same mode, he would have given to all the same inclinations and conceptions: but he has wisely ordered it otherwise, that piety and virtue might increase by an honest emulation of religions, as industry in trade, or activity in a race, from the mutual emulation of the candidates for wealth and honour."[1] This was too liberal and extensive a plan, to meet the approbation of a greedy and ambitious clergy, whose object was to establish a hierarchy for themselves,

[1] Symmach. *Ep.* 10 & 61. Themist. *Orat ad Imperat.*

rather than to procure happiness for others. It was accordingly condemned with vehemence and success by Ambrosius, Prudentius, and other orthodox leaders of the age.

It was from the ancient system of emanations, that the general hospitality which characterised the manners of the heroic ages, and which is so beautifully represented in the *Odyssey* of Homer, in a great measure arose. The poor, and the stranger who wandered in the street and begged at the door, were supposed to be animated by a portion of the same divine spirit which sustained the great and powerful. *They are all from Jupiter*, says Homer, *and a small gift is acceptable.*[1] This benevolent sentiment has been compared by the English commentators to that of the Jewish moralist, who says, *that he who giveth to the poor lendeth to the Lord, who will repay him tenfold.*[2] But it is scarcely possible for anything to be more different: Homer promises no other reward for charity than the benevolence of the action itself; but the Israelite holds out that which has always been the great motive for charity among his countrymen— the prospect of being repaid ten-fold. They are always ready to show their bounty upon such incen-

[1] *Odyss.* ζ, ver. 207.
[2] See Pope's *Odyssey.*

tives, if they can be persuaded that they are founded upon good security. It was the opinion, however, of many of the most learned among the ancients, that the principles of the Jewish religion were originally the same as those of the Greek, and that their God was no other than the creator and generator Bacchus,[1] who, being viewed through the gloomy medium of the hierarchy, appeared to them a jealous and irascible God; and so gave a more austere and unsociable form to their devotion. The golden vine preserved in the temple at Jerusalem,[2] and the taurine forms of the cherubs, between which the Deity was supposed to reside, were symbols so exactly similar to their own, that they naturally concluded them meant to express the same ideas; especially as there was nothing in the avowed principles of the Jewish worship to which they could be applied. The ineffable name also, which, according to the Massorethic punctuation, is pronounced *Jehovah,* was anciently pronounced *Jaho,* Ιαω, or Ιευω,[3] which was a title of Bacchus, the nocturnal sun;[4] as was

[1] Tacit. *Histor.* lib. v.

[2] The vine and goblet of Bacchus are also the usual devices upon the Jewish and Samaritan coins, which were struck under the Asmonean kings.

[3] Hieron. *Comm. in Psalm.* viii. Dioidor. Sic. lib. i. Philo-Bybl. *ap. Euseb. Prep. Evang.* lib. i. c. ix.

[4] Macrob. *Sat.* lib. i. c. xviii.

also *Sabazius,* or *Sabadius,*[1] which is the same word as *Sabbaoth,* one of the scriptural titles of the true God, only adapted to the pronunciation of a more polished language. The Latin name for the Supreme God belongs aiso to the same root; Ιυ-πατηρ, Jupiter, signifying Father Ιευ, though written after the ancient manner, without the dipthong, which was not in use for many ages after the Greek colonies settled in Latium, and introduced the Arcadian alphabet. We find St. Paul likewise acknowledging, that the Jupiter of the poet Aratus was the God whom he adored;[2] and Clemens of Alexandria explains St. Peter's prohibition of worshipping after the manner of the Greeks, not to mean a prohibition of worshipping the same God, but merely of the corrupt mode in which he was then worshipped.[3]

---

[1] Macrob. *Sat.* lib. i. c. xviii.
[2] *Act. Apost.* c. xvii. ver. 28.
[3] Stramat. lib. v.

www.ingramcontent.com/pod-product-compliance
Lightning Source LLC
Chambersburg PA
CBHW022105280326
41933CB00007B/262